FLORENCIA CERRUTI

Rebirth at 50

In the end,
it was not *The End*

Translated by Marie Perry

Rebirth at 50: In the end, it was not *The End*

First Spanish edition: November 2018

Third print in Spanish: January 2020

First print in English: August 2020

Original title: Renacer a los 50: la enfermedad de Parkinson como punto de partida

Cover design by: Elisa Varela

ISBN: 978-9915-40-072-3

Acknowledgments

I will be forever grateful to the hundreds of readers of the Spanish version, for their feedback, for their encouragement to continue, for making me understand how important it is to keep sharing and inspiring others. I never imagined what would happen after I published *Renacer a los 50: la enfermedad de Parkinson como punto de partida*. I thought I was writing to help others, and I realized that I was the one who benefited the most. Thank you, gentle readers, for helping me to find a meaning in life.

I would like to acknowledge Eloisa Dudok and Erika Strand for their contribution to the first milestone in the translation of this book. I am deeply grateful for their encouragement to have an English version.

I would specially need to express my gratitude to Marie Perry, for her commitment to our «project», for her patience towards my perfectionism, for always having a smile for me. We have become close friends. She wrote this poem during the process of the translation.

«*Two women, two different languages*

Two warriors, two different countries

Two dreams, two different time zones

Two sets of symptoms, two different Parkinson's

Two women that dreamt, two dreams that will come true

One feeling of confluence, as together we fly, our dreams to find

Together with one goal: To reach out through Florencia's experiences captured in her book, assuring Parkinson's patients that they are not alone in the wining road. Dream because dreams do come true».

Table of contents

Poem
Don´t give up

Don´t give up, you still have time, to reach up and start anew, / accept your shadows, bury your fears, / free your burdens, fly again. / Don´t give up, that's what life is, / continue the journey, chase your dreams, / unstick time, move the rubble / and uncover the sky.

Don t give up, please don't give in, / even if the cold burns, / even if fear bites, / even if the sun sets and the wind goes silent. / There is still fire in your soul, there is still life in your dreams.

Because life is yours and yours is the desire, / because you have loved it and because I love you, / because wine exists and love is true.

Because there are no wounds that time doesn't heal. / To open the doors, take away the locks, / abandon the walls that have protected you, / to live life and accept the challenge.

Get laughter back, practice a song, / lower your guard and extend your hands, / open your wings and try again, / celebrate life and take back the skies.

Don´t give up, please don't give in, / even if the cold burns, even if fear bites, / even if the sun sets, and the wind goes silent. / There is still fire in your soul, there is still life in your dreams.

Because every day is a new beginning, / because this is the time and the best moment / because you are not alone / because I love you.

Author unknown

Prologue

A handbook for those diagnosed with Parkinson's (or any other disease of this magnitude), for their families, for those who work in the health sector (in both policy and service provision), for society; an in-depth letter, a psychological essay, a beautiful and sparkling tale of poetry; at times personal confessions, at others, a call for attention to society's treatment of disability and the disabled, a sociological note... *Rebirth at 50* is all this and much more.

It is also - and because of my affinity with the subject, I highlight it - the clearest example of how the written word heals and projects positively. «As soon as I began to write I realized that I had discovered the most remarkable therapeutic tool». Nothing could be more evident throughout the pages of a book that deserves the widest distribution worldwide, as the dramas that its pages reveal are universal. And with no doubt, the author's degree of resilience would echo in that same proportion.

Rebirth at 50 was the driving force for someone who knew she was on the hero's path, in the mythical sense of the expression. The author is a heroine who, though still barely aware of the adventure that would require her to deploy all her resources, surrounded herself with allies and recognized enemies. By converting obstacles into positive forces, she constantly transforms enemies into challenges, into opportunities for growth. The journey of this heroine was presented to me in an ocean at times calm, at times turbulent, agitated. Does she know what the ultimate destination is? Not for sure, but I feel she cares little as long as the aim is the day, the now, the most immediate present. To reject the future in favor of the present day is perhaps the most exquisite temporal bet that we can make.

Lucid, tender, profound and social, the book's story immersed me in the author's intimacy and, thanks to her professional perspective that infuses many of the pages, also immersed me in the society's kitchen, where both compassion and prejudice are cooked; the warm hand as well as bewilderment towards others' illness; service as ignorance and superstition.

I am convinced that if we read between the lines of *Rebirth at 50*, our age or physical condition would not matter: the reading would force us to rethink our lives and consider whether it is time for each of us to rebirth. To describe the book as being about a specific disease would be a petty act for both readers and people. Florencia brings us face to face with a much deeper issue.

What good did Parkinson's disease bring to me? asks Florencia. I think a new purpose in life. Or maybe *the* purpose of her life. One that, like an enormous hug, embraces and puts us all in front of a mirror in the most loving, honest, and transparent way.

What good did Florencia's Parkinson's bring us? A book that is a door to the intimacy of people who experience that disease, hundreds of questions, the responsibility to find answers and act accordingly; it brought us a sincere, raw, warm story; the certainty of being in front of someone who before the disease perhaps did not recognize her literary gifts or her power for resilience, to rebirth.

«Everything tells me that the way forward is through renewal», says Florencia in one of my favorite chapters: *The vines shake to the beat of the tarot.* Nothing clearer in her case. Nothing clearer for each reader who decides to make his vines tremble.

Ariel Puyelli

Writer and journalist

Foreword

Why am I writing this? I know this question will come. Also, that of for whom am I writing. The answers will emerge throughout the reading.

The first impulse came after an appointment with the neurologist in which he said to me: «You are very informed; it is not common that patients absorb all the information you have». On the way home, an idea developed in my head: I would share all my information. What I had read, what I had researched and discovered, what I had thought about, but also what I had been living and feeling.

Writing is not new to me. In fact, I have published several books and articles. But in this new project, there were two novel elements. The first was that I wouldn't do it as a part of a team, the way I usually work; this time I would have to face the challenge on my own. And the second was that I wouldn't write about nutrition, lifestyles or early childhood. I would open my heart and reveal the most intimate and deep aspects of myself that I had come to know.

I was eager to get started. Once at home, the first pages flowed with desperation. I realized that I had discovered the most remarkable therapeutic tool. I read that this is particularly the case for perfectionists like me, because every word or feeling written responds to a careful decision about whether it is the right one...or the perfect one. My therapist says that she is amazed not to find a single superfluous word. This is because each sentence reflects several months of intense thought.

I write as I face new experiences, to express my feelings with precision and record the process, about both facts and emotions. I write in my head, especially while I exercise or drive. When I get to the keyboard, it's just a matter of transcribing. I love to do it in the dawn's calm when everyone else is asleep. My husband once asked me: «What time of the day do you write?».

A few months ago I received an email promoting a workshop called *Writing to Heal*. Accustomed to a succession of events impossible to attribute to chance, I knew immediately that I had to take it. In fact, I write to heal myself…

I write because I like to.

I write because it makes me well.

I write to clarify my feelings.

I write to put into words what not everyone can.

I write to commit myself to my decisions.

I write to share tools, resources, and lessons learned.

I write to explain to others how to be with me.

But deep down, I write to heal myself.

Preface
Touched by an evil fairy...
or was it a fairy godmother?

Not so long ago, someone who hadn't seen me for 20 years, told me that she remembered me as «a strong, dedicated, intelligent, creative, determined and hardworking person». I would add controlling, perfectionist, demanding, self-sufficient and as a boss once said to me, «not very humble»...

Sometimes I think if someone wanted to give me the biggest lesson of my life, they couldn't have done better than to send me Parkinson's disease at 47. One morning, as I walked down the *rambla*, I thought I might as well create a fairy tale to distill down the disease's meaning for me, imagining an evil fairy had touched me.

And I imagined the evil fairy gave me a single touch with her magic wand, with which she passed me Parkinson's disease. A single touch, followed by four questions, was enough to teach me the big lesson I needed to learn.

The fairy said to me: «Do you think you can have everything under your control? Well, it turns out you can't even control your right hand». Can there be anything more symbolic than losing control of your right hand?

The fairy continued: «Do you think you can achieve perfection? Well, it turns out that you are now visibly imperfect». Can there be anything symbolically more imperfect than a disability? And as visibly imperfect as Parkinson's disease?

The fairy insisted: «Do you think you can do anything you set your mind to? Then you will have to feel in your flesh what it's like to feel vulnerable». Can there be a greater feeling of vulnerability than that you experience when you know you have a disease that will limit you more and more, but you don't even know how and when will it happen? And with the particularity that it is a neurodegenerative disease.

And with no compassion the fairy finished by asking: «Do you believe that your intelligence is greater than that of the rest and are you proud of your efficiency and your ability to work? Well, now your brain images show large blue areas of neurons that don't work. Your precious brain is visibly damaged». Nothing could have been more enlightening.

And these were the four aspects that I had considered the most outstanding of my personality, on which I had built my identity and from which I drew my confidence. The evil fairy had left me at the crossroads, where I had only two paths left: to sink or to start again.

But the evil fairy didn't leave me alone. First, she took off her evil costume and revealed that she was a fairy godmother who had a very important mission for me. She chose a few angels to join me on my difficult journey, provided the information I would need in the most incredible ways, and enrolled me, without asking for my permission, in many difficult and intensive courses on life that I would not otherwise have taken. And thus, a painful, yet ultimately enriching process, ensued. I called it «my 50 renewal».

The fairy told me I had the gift of being able to put my feelings and experiences into words. And that these gifts come with responsibilities. So, she asked me to share my story with those who need them.

These pages are the most honest I have ever written. I wrote them with complete freedom, with no desire to please anyone other than my heart. Readers will find in them my successes and my mistakes on a path that led me to rediscover myself. There are no shortcuts, nor recipes. But as a taxi driver with tears in his eyes concluded as he listened to my story: «Then there's an "after"». If, when reading these pages, someone can find relief, hope or a reflection from which to draw inspiration, then I will have achieved my goal. And these intense and difficult years will have had a meaning.

Four years ago the interpretation of my numbers at birth - according to Tantric numerology – left me perplexed. This reading clearly stated that my mission in life was to deliver a message of hope: «If Florencia did it, it is possible». From that time to this part I have continued to receive innumerable and unmistakable signs confirming this mission. If this is so, I dedicate these pages to those who need to receive them.

PART I

«Stop the world;
I want to get off»

June 2014 – February 2016

I started writing this first part almost a year after my diagnosis and it leads you through to the beginning of the acceptance stage. This phase embeds the impact of the news, the identification of the fears, and the realization that I was facing a major challenge, which implied recognizing that I had to rediscover myself as the only way I could move forward. How much easier it would have been if I could have gotten off of the world, as Mafalda - the character of the Argentinian cartoonist Quino- implored, as if it were a ride that could stop. Not forever... just for a little while... time enough to think calmly and come back knowing what to do, avoiding mistakes. But no, this whole intense experience took place while life went on, as a parallel process was taking place in my loved ones, as I kept working, while my responsibilities didn't give me a break...

My first year with «the Englishman»

June 2014

The diagnosis of Parkinson's disease when I was 47 years old touched even the most remote of my cells.

I never asked myself: «Why me?». I wondered what I would do with my life with a neurodegenerative, chronic and so far incurable disease. A friend of mine told me: «It hits you where it hurts the most». I completely agree.

My life was always a cult of perfection, of intelligence, of work, of efficiency. Disability didn't have a place among these pillars. Also, I never really got along with disability. I always controlled, or pretended to control, everything that was going on around me. Now I panic when I feel I lose control of my body. My husband says that I refill the water in the *mate* as if I have fear; I explain to him that although I give my hands the same order, each one arrives at a different time to the position where I want them to; I don't control the speed of the movements so I refill the *mate* slowly, with fear.

Fear is the key word that summarizes everything I feel. Maybe I should say terror. I get terrified as I go through the list of symptoms because I find them humiliating. I am especially terrified of their visibility. I also identify the fear of losing my independence, the fear of not being able to work efficiently, the fear of looking like a person with a disability, the fear of losing my intelligence, the fear of not being able to face a group of students... And I go much further; I worry about who will take care of me whenever I need it. According to my therapist, I want to control what might happen in thirty years. Which probably will never happen. That's what I was doing in those first forty-seven years.

Ruediger Dahlke, doctor and psychotherapist, in his book *The Healing Power of Illness,* writes something that struck me:

The lesson that patients [with Parkinson's disease] must learn is redemption, that is, the realization of the pattern manifested in the symptoms. Therefore, it is about taking smaller steps, settling for less, not raising your voice so loudly, and paying attention to the slight details that are required. It is necessary not to focus so much on quantity as on quality, the nuances are of paramount importance.

I realize the disease came to me with a purpose and that it is up to me to figure it out.

I didn't cry when I got the diagnosis. I cried a couple of months before when, after describing my symptoms to my endocrinologist, she raised her eyebrows a few millimeters while she referred me to the neurologist. That day I had the certainty that something was wrong and that whatever it was, it was serious. I couldn't hold back my tears. At the second appointment with the neurologist, I came in with the results of several studies that ruled out other diseases and having spent several long hours reading, trying to find the cause of my symptoms. The diagnosis didn't surprise me. It was my husband who was shocked. He was by my side when I received the news. He was sure there was nothing wrong with me, that all I was noticing was a natural consequence of aging and that I was exaggerating. Other doctors had already said it was stress or depression. We left the neurologist's office in silence. I collected the medications I had to start taking, under the complicit gaze of the staff, and we left... He took me to get dinner makings at the mall supermarket! And in the corridor of that mall, my husband hugged me. But it wasn't until much later that we could talk about it.

Infinite thoughts and impertinent questions - for which I had no answer - flooded my head for the first days. They rattled at full speed, in and out, and then in and out again, as no answer or solution ever appeared. The thoughts were so intense that they left no room for crying or talking about my feelings. The first time I cried after the diagnosis was during an appointment with the psychiatrist, around a month later. She pointed out that I had arrived late and she told me she didn't know if she could see me. I struck back with all the evidence that I had arrived on time. Not only had I arrived on time, but I had crossed the city to arrive breathless for my appointment at one o'clock. And I wasn't late but, as other patients had not shown up, the time of my appointment had been brought forward. She finally agreed to see me. I cried while I told her about the diagnosis. Those were tears summoned by the feeling of unfairness. That day marked a turning point in my relationship with my psychiatrist, for the better.

I had a brain scan after the diagnosis. In the beginning, the technician said to me: «You're too young for this», and when he finished, he asked me if I had any children. In response to my answer, he said: «Luckily they're grown-ups now». I hadn't yet thought about this and I doubt he realized the effect that those 6 words would have on me. My boss, who is a doctor, joined me to pick up the results. I had to gather a lot of courage to read the report and see the images that the technician had seen. Several parts of my brain colored in blue showed areas of low activity. This test didn't change the diagnosis but *seeing* it was something else. Sometimes my boss tells me to remember everything she told me at the time, but I was in shock; my memories are vague.

In the early days, I immersed myself in hyperactivity that bordered on mania. I jumped out of bed at dawn and began to clean up, tidy up, and throw away everything that didn't work. I didn't stop all day and didn't feel tired. My eldest daughter asked: «What's going on? Why is everything so clean it shines?». I started making plans to sell my beloved house and move into an apartment. My husband looked at me worriedly. One day he found me at eleven o'clock at night cleaning the bathroom grate and asked: «Is this necessary?». When I described the situation to a doctor he said that it seemed like my reaction to wanting to start over. And I think he was right. I've felt like a teenager, trying to figure out who I am, what I like to do, what's good for me, what physical activity I prefer, who I want to be. There's a song by José Luis Perales that says: «It's not easy to forget everything and start all over again». He refers to love, but I often find myself humming it. Especially the verses that say «it's not easy…».

No one can believe my diagnosis and I chose not to mention it anymore. At first, I felt compelled to tell my family, my friends, my co-workers. I only shared it with people with whom I had an emotional connection, whether they were friends or colleagues. In some ways this made it easier for me; I didn't have to explain why I went to the doctor so often or why I was sometimes feeling under the weather or didn't perform at my usual level. At work, I was a disaster: I couldn't concentrate, I had trouble deciding, and I would forget everything. I don't know what I would have done without the support of my colleagues. By spending so many hours a day with them, they were more aware of what was happening to me and how I felt than my own family and closest friends. But when I interviewed a student who didn't take her eyes off my hands for an entire meeting, I realized that the news had taken on a gossip character, and I didn't feel good about it. And I felt that it didn't help me at all for my students to know about my disease. What's more, I find it difficult to establish a teacher-student relationship under these conditions. I am no longer in control of this situation, and I still don't know how I want to handle it. I should have asked for discretion to those who I shared my diagnosis with, to give me time to digest the news, but I didn't.

I didn't expect the way people reacted when I shared the news of my diagnosis. There was a bit of everything: disbelief, support, and incredibly varied offers of help. Some changed the subject quickly. I could even say that there was denial from some of them. But there were also tears, and I found myself comforting loved ones, a situation for which I was not prepared, it was very odd...

It destabilized me to hear that there could be a misdiagnosis and that instead of Parkinson's I could have a reversible disease. Nor was it good for me to listen to others saying that miracles happen. I thought: «Who am I to deserve a miracle?». Each day it took monumental effort to set out on the path of acceptance, and these ideas unbalanced me.

I realized that I was the one who had to tell others what I needed and how they could help me, but I still didn't have the answer. And, since I wasn't sure, I locked myself in, trying to keep me safe as I figured it out and processed everything that was happening to me. But protection has the cost of depriving you of the love of people you don't let in, and I felt that. I knew I didn't want my disease to be the topic of conversation every time I met someone; I didn't want to talk about it in public or in a group because it made me crumble emotionally and I still had to face the rest of the day; I didn't want to feel observed; I wanted to get people to see Parkinson's through me and not me through Parkinson's. I didn't want — then or now — the disease to define me.

My mother was the only one who didn't need many explanations. She phoned me the day after I received the diagnosis and noticed something different in my voice. She asked: «Is something wrong?». And without sugar-coating it at all, I replied: «Yesterday my neurologist told me I have Parkinson's disease». And when she asked me how she could help me, at the age of 47 years old, I found myself answering:

«Pamper me». The healing power of a mother's love goes beyond age and time. And she understood perfectly what I needed from her. She invites me to have tea and brings me presents from everywhere. I, who was never very devout, saw how my bedroom filled up with angels, little virgins, crosses, medals, blessed oils...

At night I look with fondness at a little straw angel hanging from the chandelier in my bedroom and I think about how many angels have appeared in my life in these months and how lucky I am. My mother did something else that was simple but brilliant. She asked me bluntly if I would prefer her not to ask me about the disease when we met and I replied I preferred not to, but we agreed that I would keep her updated on everything she needed to know.

In these months I've noticed the number of times a day people ask you «How are you?». I think 99 percent of people expect you to say: «Fine, and you?». So many times, I would have wanted to answer: «Not well», and other times I would have wanted to talk about what was happening to me. But I know that people don't always want to hear about other people's problems. I think as long as they keep asking me «How are you?», I will go on answering: «Fine, thank you». I need another clue to know how much they want to hear.

I started reading about Parkinson's like crazy. My psychiatrist recommended against it. I followed her advice for a while but inevitably came back to the reading. At first, I wanted to understand, to know what I would face, what the expected evolution was, the prognosis, the life expectancy, the probability of complications. One of the first things I read was a booklet that had all kinds of rehabilitation techniques for patients with Parkinson's. With horror, I read about therapies to improve swallowing and speech, intellectual disorders, about constipation, and countless other symptoms. I read and told my husband: «Gustavo, this is horrible!», and he, who is very pragmatic, would say: «If it makes you feel bad to read it, why do you keep doing it?».

Reading about the disease allowed me to recognize signs of Parkinson's in me that began several years earlier. I read that the disease begins long before motor symptoms are noticeable. Some people talk about eight years, and others even more. Twenty years ago (I wonder if it's possible) my brother laughed at how I moved my arms when I ran. Five years ago, when I was looking at the 15th birthday party photos of my youngest daughter, I got mad at the makeup woman, because my skin was shiny, and that hadn't happened at my oldest daughter´s celebration, four years before, with the same makeup woman. I can't remember how long it's been since I started smelling less than other people, but it's been for many years. Once I traveled with my husband on a bus with a band of musicians who had played the entire night, and he complained the whole way about their body odor. The smell didn't exist for me. But I can't either enjoy the smell of cinnamon any more, as I used to do. It also brought back memories of the apple cakes my mother used to cook when I was a little girl. I changed the brand of cinnamon that I buy several times. I didn't understand why I couldn't smell the scent and thought the company was misleading consumers by mixing the cinnamon with another powder to lower production costs. I speak very softly, every day more so. I eat slowly. My daughters have for a long time made fun of how long I take to eat.

For many years I have also suffered from sleep disorders and the only response I had from health care providers was recommendations on sleep hygiene that didn't help me at all. I spent many years sleeping badly and taking hypnotic or sleeping pills –feeling guilty- when I couldn't resist insomnia anymore. I read that anyone with sleep disorders should be asked if they have a loss of smell, as someone with these two conditions should be thoroughly evaluated to identify a diagnosis of Parkinson's before motor symptoms appear. I've had symptoms of depression for years too; I remember looking at people in the supermarket and thinking: «What are they laughing at?». Going to the supermarket isn't my favorite hobby either...

Overall, I'm fine today, and my disease doesn't keep me from doing anything important. The medication I'm taking helps me write better and I no longer feel like I'm dragging my tongue when I speak, but I still find it difficult to make some precise movements. It gets more complicated in the mornings. I had never noticed how many of these fine movements I need to do at that time of day. Buttons, zippers, clips, necklaces, earrings, belts, wallets, keys, locks, pockets... They are all together waiting to challenge you as soon as you get up. And if I feel stressed, I lose the battle before I even start.

Hooking a bra with a back closure when you're in a hurry is simply mission impossible. The club physiotherapist recommends not to stop doing these fine movements. She told me: «Keep trying harder; don't take the easy way». This would mean to simplify my tasks by wearing T-shirts instead of blouses, shoes without laces, accessories that need not to be pinned on. I get the message. Luckily, she explained to me that hooking the back closure of a bra is hard on the shoulders and that no one should do it.

I think the most reasonable approach is what I had intuitively started to do anyway: set the alarm clock one hour earlier and do everything calmly and without stress. That way there's nothing I cannot do. The only user-friendly adjustment I made was to get an electric toothbrush because I couldn't clean my teeth properly, and my lifelong dentist — after the corresponding shock — recommended to alternate it with a regular one. I also cannot wash my hair well and it's hard for me to untangle it; I cut it shorter, and that helped a bit.

Until now the disease has not affected my balance. I always enjoyed doing balancing postures during yoga practice and I have photos doing the tree pose in front of inspiring landscapes on every trip I've made with my childhood friends. A few days ago, I put one of these photos as a background on the office computer to remind me to take care of my inner balance and work on maintaining the physical one. I want to continue making the tree pose in front of the landscapes that inspire me.

I read about intellectual disorders, memory, and attention span. I identified with the fact that people with Parkinson's have a better chance of recalling old memories than recent ones. It was something that had always caught my attention in my piano lessons. My mother taught me when I was a child. As a teenager, I took classes for several years with a teacher. In one of the annual exams, I got a highly applauded ovation and grade after having played the complete *Fur Elise*, by Beethoven, from memory. A few years later, however, I remembered only one part: the one that my mother had taught me when I was not even ten years old.

My therapist, who is not at all conventional, suggested I do a body- consciousness exercise. I was shocked to find out that I didn't recognize my right arm as my own. I felt it like a rigid metal prosthesis. It was not part of my body. Going a little deeper, I felt that I had abandoned it, and when I got that feeling, I wanted to take it in and love it. The next day, in my tai-chi practice, the teacher said to me: «Move your hands with more intention, Florencia; you are letting them drop». I think tai-chi practice will help me bring my right arm back into my body.

There was a time, just before the diagnosis, when my GP prescribed antidepressants. Not only did I feel better than ever before, but I also saw that everything around me improved as my body responded favorably to the medication. But that didn't last long, because they were incompatible with a Parkinson's medication that I started taking afterward. That was a difficult stage. On the one hand, because I was facing my recent diagnosis. But also, and this is hard for people who do not agree on taking antidepressants to understand, people with Parkinson's may be depressed just because of the chemical imbalances in the brain resulting from the lack of neurotransmitters. Therapy and exercise can help, but they are not always enough.

I've realized that going to the doctor — to any doctor — will be a nightmare from now on. I see the optician for an eyeglass prescription, and she orders two new tests because my eye convergence is failing. There are so many muscles involved in vision... I come to the dermatologist so she can check a mole and learn I am a patient at risk of melanoma, and she wants to see me more often. I go to the otolaryngologist and he checks my vocal cords, to identify the cause of my dysphonia. My GP questions the diagnosis and wants to talk to my neurologist. Now I´m not in the condition to answer «Yes» to the traditional question of whether I am healthy; every professional I go to, will see me as a high-risk patient. It is exhausting.

People laugh or get angry at the symptoms as if you´re doing it on purpose. «Can't you speak louder? I cannot hear you». «I'm exasperated at how slowly you eat». «Is it a pain that you are always tired?». I left other people speechless. Before I had a diagnosis, I remember telling a colleague I found it hard to write, and she, one who talks your ear off, said: «I don't know what to say». Even people who know about my disease get annoyed with the symptoms. I think it has to do with the fact that I'm young, vital, and that I don't look like a sick person. And with the fact that people around me don't want me to be sick.

I often witness how people mock the elderly and impaired by imitating hand tremors. And I think I cannot even reproduce it, because I've become very clumsy doing fast, repetitive movements like sprinkling, adding salt, greeting, imitating the tremors. And that hurts me. It also hurts when I hear people joking and saying: «The German man showed up» when they forget something. Those who joke about this surely do not understand what it's like to cope with the diagnosis of a neurodegenerative, chronic, and incurable disease. Some people call Parkinson's «the Englishman». I hope that one day I will be able to joke about «the Englishman» with permission of those who live with him and not from the mockery of those who do not.

I couldn't face the day I turned 48. My birthday parties were a January tradition, in which I offered my friends a display of delicious dishes I cooked. This year I couldn't. I went to work, just like every day, and in the afternoon I holed up in my garden, making 60 cuttings of my ivy vine to give to a friend. With such concentration and intensity, as if life itself depended on it. I hope to see them grow in my friend's garden and remember that day as a stage I overcame.

A co-worker told me I didn't have a disease, but a condition. And I kept thinking about it because the idea sounded attractive to me. But I think I do have a disease, which name is Parkinson's disease, that can affect the most unimaginable muscles, and that if I don't face it, it can take over my body. I am not willing to let that happen. It is one thing to accept the disease and another to surrender. That's why I try to do all my homework.

I know that taking my medication every day at the right time is a key factor. And on Sunday mornings I prepare the pill dispensers for the week, so I don't forget to take any of those pills and I can detect in time what I have to refill soon. I do it with aversion because there are so many pills, but at the same time, I appreciate all the medication available nowadays that improves the quality of life for people with Parkinson's. And my other important duty is to exercise regularly. I do tai-chi, which is especially good for improving the stability of people with Parkinson's, something for which the medication isn't as effective. I also do muscle-strengthening exercises in the fitness room because my neurologist told me that my body has to be in excellent physical condition, and I'm slowly making some progress. Besides, I walk or run depending on the pain in my knee. I discovered that while I do physical activity, the stiffness — especially that of my legs —fades away. I feel free and the endorphins I release make me feel great.

Sometimes I feel like Forrest Gump, I feel like I want to keep running and never stop. Only while I am running, occasionally I will shed a few tears of rage. No professor comes to talk to me while I run. I think my body language must be very clear. Although I believe that my body language has always said: «Keep your distance».

My therapist says it would be good for me to hit something, or to scratch out lines on a piece of paper, but my parents taught me to be correct and prudent first, and those reactions don't fit. At least for now. On Saturdays, I go with no rush to the club and sometimes I ask the teachers in the fitness room what else I can do, and they say: «It's OK, Flor; go home and rest». And that reminds me of how a friend of mine and I used to laugh because she is called by her nickname even at the bank; now it's happening to me too.

When I told another co-worker about all the tasks I have to do, she said: «You have to dedicate yourself to the disease». And I think the word *dedicate* is perfect. You can't leave it for whatever time you have left after doing everything else. That doesn't work. You're so tired that you won't do it. You have to schedule the disease-related tasks as if they were the most important meetings. I read that people with Parkinson's get better when they moderate their workload. And that's because they give themselves time to take care of the disease (or *dedicate* themselves to it), and because stress makes all the symptoms worse. And I would also add tiredness, nervousness, and intense emotions.

I sum up the hours a week I dedicate to it and they are many. The programmed ones, the just *fifteen-minute health tasks* indicated by several specialists, and the ones that nobody counts: those you spend doing everything a little slower. There are also the hours dedicated to thinking and reflecting which add more than all the others together. I would like to incorporate dance, swimming, and meditation, but I still can't find time for them.

In a second stage, I began to read so I could act. And I went on to research scientific literature. There I came across research on Parkinson's and tai-chi, I understood why weight loss occurs; I delved into neuroprotective foods, in the association between pesticides and the disease, the particularities of a healthy diet for a Parkinson's patient, and alternatives to slow the disease's rate of progress.

I have a degree in Nutrition and I want to help. Selfishly, I want to help. I remember what I heard the Chilean psychologist Pilar Sordo says: «Happiness is giving». It's that simple. I believe that I will feel a lot better when I can get out of my cage and help others with my knowledge, from my limitless reading, and my own experiences. In July it will be a year since my diagnosis. I don't know if I'm ready, but I want to point myself in that direction. Nothing gives me more satisfaction than teaching, than interacting with people. I also like to write. The first thing I want to do is to organize everything I've read and thought about and try to write something that could be useful to other people with this disease. And when I get to feel stronger, maybe I could share it publicly.

«Let yourself flow», said the card I was dealt during a meeting with my friends. The words touched me. I feel that this is what I am doing at this moment. Every word I let flow gives me a little more relief.

My husband gets mad because I can't stop thinking about the disease. And he's right. But for the time being, I can't avoid thinking about it, no matter how hard I try. My hands remind me of it at every moment. I have two options: either I try to fill my head with something else and spend hours advancing in Candy Crush game or tirelessly looking at online shopping options, or I can let my head think about Parkinson's productively. I chose the latter.

My therapist says I'm entering the acceptance stage. It fills me with joy.

The first phase ends: the unclosure

December 2014

Only when I could feel that I had made some progress towards accepting the disease, did I perceive that some sort of inner wall began to crumble. It was a transparent yet impenetrable wall; I could see through it, but I couldn't reach what was on the other side. I knew it blocked me from others´ feelings and worries about what was happening to me; that they had to process it too and that they also had their problems; but I couldn't get there. I hadn't raised it consciously, rather I believe that my self-preservation instinct built it. I needed that time of insight. They were months of handling many emotions, of much meditation, of recording all the words and gestures, of thinking and thinking. And that was more than I could handle. Crossing the wall was not an option.

Something similar happens when the computer screen shows a function you can't click on it, because there are conditions that you haven't fulfilled yet or steps that you have to take previously. And when you meet those prerequisites, you can click on it, the function changes its color, and from that moment on it is possible to execute that command. That's how I felt it: I saw the function but a greater force than the forces of will or duty unabled me to take the next step until I was ready.

But one day I felt that magically and suddenly that wall was no longer there. And I began to concern myself again with other people's emotions and give them permission to enter and know mine. I started thinking about how my mother, my husband, my daughters, my sister, my brothers, my friends had felt over the preceding months.

I was touched to know that others had been suffering for me, but even more so they had felt upset because I did not allow them to be involved in my process, or that I did not let them help me in the way they wanted to.

My mother was the first person I spoke with. She told me how hard it had been for her. She worried and prayed while going through her own process. At the end of that year, while preparing the traditional family dinner, she felt a gush come up through her throat and out of her body as a hoarse and deep voice. It was not her voice, and it said: «Thy will be done».

I thanked her for making me so strong and for all the values I received from her and to which I could count on. When we finished, it surprised me to be the one who gave her the certainty and peace of mind that I would be fine. She invited me to spend a few days together in Buenos Aires. We laughed, cried, talked, and walked for five days. One of those days I asked her: «What am I humming?», and she replied: «A lullaby». We chatted and talked about what I was writing but still had shown no one. I feel that our consciousnesses communicate. I also feel that those days were very healing for both of us. This trip marked the beginning of a new stage.

I went over the values and resources I had at my disposal. The first was my perfectionism, at this time in conflict. It allowed me to detect what neither my husband nor several doctors could notice. Second, determination and perseverance; I didn't stop until I came up with a diagnosis. But also my determination to face the matter head-on. Discipline, to concentrate on what I had to do. Responsibility, to my body, and to those who love me. Strength; I can stand up every time I fall. Creative skills and self-motivation. Endurance. And why not, intelligence? But above all, my greatest resource is knowing that I am surrounded by people who love me and a lot. Unconditionally.

It is well known that tough times put couples through the ringer. In our case, we came out stronger. I am touched to see the love my husband showed me. Not in words, but in gestures. When we got married, I was a 23-year-old girl and he was a 30-year-old man. I constantly bombarded him with silly questions like, «do you love me?», «what do you like most about me?». Once he answered the latter: «That you are so hardworking». I never asked again. And I learned that men's love, at least my husband's, cannot be measured by words or gifts. It should be measured by gestures. And in these tough times, my husband joined me in everything.

He goes with me to the neurologist with more commitment than for my prenatal appointments. He protects me from everything that hurts me and I have seen him get furious in my defense. He watches me without me even noticing and without saying a word. He makes me react when necessary. He agreed to help sell the house until one day he could make me see it was just a crazy idea. He took on everything I didn't have the strength to do or the will. If it had been up to me, I would have gone to bed without dinner for months, but he took care of it. However, now he is asking for me again in the kitchen, he must see I am feeling better... I often wonder what I would have done if he hadn't been by my side. When I told him I had been writing my experiences, he looked at me with a horrified expression, but when I explained to him the good it did to me and I gave him pages to read, he hugged me and supported me, as he always does.

I shyly began to share the first drafts of my experiences with some of my relatives and I wrote a brief message to each of them. I did it little by little because their responses overwhelmed me and I needed to dilute the emotions. Only one loved friend said she wanted to wait until she got the feeling to read it. Although she later explained the meaning of her words, it was so great a blow I hesitated on continuing to share my work. But I kept doing it, and I was happy with this decision. Love gushed for me in return. People told me they felt honored and privileged that I had chosen them to share something so intimate. They thanked me for having sent them such honest experiences, based on our shared humanity. My words awoke an amalgam of feelings: emotion, pain, rebellion, impotence, solidarity, grief, pride, gratitude, admiration, bewilderment over knowing feelings of mine I had never shown...

They helped me make sense of what was happening to me: «You connected with the best of you»; «you are encountering an unexplored part of yourself»; «always rigid, organized, moderate, introverted, how did you never allow yourself the chance to be you? Where did you keep all this?»; «God willing, when we are old ladies one day you will tell me you were happiest after your Parkinson's diagnosis»; they told me that coincidences do not exist and that everything in life happens for a reason.

I received great compliments. The comments surprised me because I didn't write seeking approval, something I had sought for a long time. However, it did me good to receive this praise. They told me I was a great woman, brave, wise, strong, brilliant, incredible, with extraordinary sensitivity... But they also told me they were sure that I would handle this situation and that they knew that I would be fine... And all these words gave me a feeling of enormous responsibility towards those who trust that it will be that way.

Many readers want to receive the next chapters. They believe that I am just scratching the surface, that it does me good, but that it can also help other people with and without Parkinson's disease. «You should publish these pages; they are extraordinary». They told me that writing is therapeutic, but that it is also a way to transcend oneself.

But finally, they gave me something that I especially needed and it was the peace of mind that they could continue seeing me as myself, regardless of the symptoms: «When I look at you I see the person I love, I see your heart and your mind; I see our shared history»; «you are a person who teaches with a conversation, with an opinion, with a gesture, with or without tremors»; «the soul does not know about perfections or exactitudes».

Revealing myself in front of others, far from making me vulnerable, made me powerful. Powerful enough to gain the trust of others and know they want to hear what I have to say. My mother and some friends often tell me I am very wise, but going through this process gave me something much stronger to reach out to others: the ability to connect with their pain, the legitimacy of someone who says something to you because he has experienced it in his flesh. Meeting face to face with those to whom I had sent the mail was so easy! I could connect with them from within, with nothing to hide, nothing to compete for, from the very essence.

When I received the diagnosis, I told each of my daughters separately, and then I invited them each for tea, also separately. I handled it the same way as when they were girls and asked about sex: I only told them what they wanted to know. The youngest, who was 18 years old, said nothing or asked questions. But the oldest, who was 22, was concerned about whether the disease could be linked to a blow to the head when I was with her. I could perceive the feeling of guilt in her gaze, obviously unjustified. We were together when a thief took my handbag, and she ran out after him, and I, in shock, after her.

No one saw nor could explain what hit me hard on the face. I chipped several teeth and deviated the septum of my nose. My eye was so swollen that I couldn't open it for days. I lost consciousness for six hours. My daughter took care of everything. She called an ambulance which never arrived. Half an hour later she took me to the car with the help of a woman who was passing by, and they took me to the ER. Then my husband came and an ambulance took me to the health facility. I had a CT scan. Meanwhile, my husband registered that I would ask every minute the same questions: «Where am I?»; «what happened to me?»; «where are the girls?». I relate all this from what my husband has told me since I remember nothing about what happened until I returned home.

The next day was one of tremendous confusion. I didn't have a cell phone, agenda, or memory. I had gaps, I would talk to someone and doubt whether I had or had not. For a long time, I had trouble remembering some things, and I sometimes had the feeling that I needed to open new mental circuits to find names in my memory. It took me a while, but I succeeded. I felt terribly insecure. I was afraid of talking to people and not remembering something important. Returning to teach was a monumental challenge. I remember that a few months later I agreed to give a lecture at an event where nobody knew me and when, after having finished, many people approached to congratulate me, I thought: «You are ready».

That accident was two years before the diagnosis and I've read a lot about the relationship between head trauma and Parkinson's disease. Some research warns that it is likely that people who develop the disease may be more likely to remember a previous episode of head trauma than those who do not have this diagnosis. Others point out that actually, the association depends more on how long the loss of consciousness lasts than on the blow itself. Anyway, I believe my illness started much earlier. But I also believe that the symptoms were triggered after that bump on the head. It wasn't until much later I could put the symptoms together. The first thing I noticed was that I spoke differently. That's why I asked my dentist if in the treatment of my cracked teeth there might have been something that made me lisp, and he replied, surprised, that there was not. Later I could see more clearly that the sensation I had was that of dragging my tongue while speaking. I also had difficulty pronouncing and finding words. A few more months later I noticed that it was hard for me to brush my teeth and wash my hair. And it was when I perceived it was difficult to write that I decided to see a doctor.

I don't know what's going on in my daughters' heads now. My husband says that nothing, because they see nothing wrong with me. And I don't want to insist either. In the meantime, I keep on doing what I used to do when they asked questions about sex.

My bedroom has continued to change. Now, besides the religious images my mother brings me, I have a Pilates ball to do the exercises for the joints that the physical therapist prescribed for me to avoid night cramps... and a hockey stick. My exercise clothes take up a bigger space in the closet. I notice my dependence on exercise, particularly because of its effect on my mood. It's like the antidepressant pill I can no longer take. There was a week when I didn't exercise because I was sick. When Sunday arrived, I couldn't stand it any longer. I locked myself in my bedroom, played music, and danced. Half an hour later, I was a different person.

When I run on the treadmill, I get desperate trying to untangle the headset so I can listen to music on my cell phone. It must sound ridiculous, but I feel like a dog that is about to get off the leash and start running. And the more anxious I am, the harder it is for me to untangle them. So I made myself a little cardboard to keep them untangled and run right away... like a dog...

I found myself speaking naturally about the disease for the first time with a colleague. Leaning in a small bookcase, we talked objectively about my weight loss and agreed on the limit at which I would put myself in her hands to make a plan to not keep losing weight. I felt such relief realizing I could speak about it naturally!

And then came the day when I could laugh at myself and at «the Englishman». My younger brother offered me some things that he would not need any more after the renovation of his house. And I am famous for taking advantage of everything, repurposing the most unthinkable things and finding a place and giving mind-blowing utility to objects that have been labeled as unusable or obsolete. It was a cruel winter's day and things were on the terrace, and with my fingers more rigid than ever because of the cold, I removed some screws about twenty centimeters long. When I entered the house, I said to my mother and my brother laughing: «Not even Parkinson's could hold me back!».

Also, and according to my therapist's predictions, my desire to work returned, although differently. It surprised me to see everything I could decide and finish in just one day. It is difficult to describe the effect of what was happening to me on my ability to decide. Parkinson's itself has its role in this, too, but I think it was more a result of the emotional issues, such as shock, stress, or depression. I confirm it by the fact that this difficulty has receded. Despite how obvious and simple a decision may be, you can't decide. And days and weeks go by, and you keep turning the decisions that are still pending around and around in your head. This was quite a blow but a great lesson. I have always been very critical of people I see as inefficient or not very dedicated to their work. And life was showing me that sometimes, even though you have the will and the abilities, you can't put them into practice.

The desire to hold meetings at home and cook also returned. First it was with my friends. It had been more than a year since we had met at home. I made waffles and we had a splendid time next to the woodstove. For that day I replaced the dingy plant on the porch with a beautiful Ficus. When I finished I realized the plant was off-center. I felt a powerful urge to dig it up, to plant it perfectly in the center. I held back while deciding that there was beauty in the blemish and that I would leave it at that. I collected red aloe flowers to put in a vase. We had discussed with my therapist about the power of this plant that blooms in the winter. As many people call me Flor (Flower in Spanish), it had a deep symbolism for me. Then I invited my co-workers to celebrate three pregnancies in the office. I realized how long it had been since I made a cake. My decorating sleeve was gone, and I hadn't even noticed it.

The ability to relax and watch a movie on the couch also came back. And I found myself one Sunday lolling around in bed at eleven o'clock in the morning... It was only once, but at that moment I realized that it was the first day in 12 months that I didn't jump out of bed.

I've experienced some strange coincidences. I read about yoga Nidra and a few days later my mother showed up with a compact disc to practice it at home. I was thinking of discussing alternatives for mood enhancement with a homeopath I know, and the next day I ran into her by chance.

I have only one very concrete fear: a freezing episode. They are temporary episodes in which for a few seconds the legs do not respond and seem to be attached to the floor. It can happen when trying to start or continue walking while changing the speed or direction of the steps. Although more common in advanced stages of the disease, one-third of people with Parkinson's experience them early on. I wonder if it will happen to me. I wonder where I will be if it happens to me and with whom. Every time I cross the *rambla* to go to work, running between cars in a place where there are no traffic lights, I wonder about it. That must be why I am increasingly choosing to go to the city center with my husband in his car, even if it means coming home later.

There's something I am mulling over in my head: sometime before the diagnosis I had a recurring memory of a vivid sensation, but I didn't know if I had dreamt it or when it was happening. In that memory, I am trying to reach someone who runs away from me and my legs do not move forward... I have asked myself many times what this memory is about. Could it be that my body registers delays of fractions of seconds between an order and its response that I do not consciously perceive? Could it be that at night while I sleep my legs do not respond? Could it be the memory of when I tried to run after my daughter and could not reach her when she was chasing after the thief? It looks similar to the description of freezing, but I had never heard of that when I had the feeling.

Now I dream of births and journeys, of journeys for which I do not have a suitcase ready and where I am about to miss the plane, but my mother shows up ready to help me gather what I need and take me to the airport... Apparently, those are signs that a new stage in my life is about to begin... a new stage that challenges me a lot. A unique journey, that of self-discovery...

The vines shake
to the beat of the tarot

When I first heard about the movie *Still Alice*, I wanted to watch it immediately. The plot revolves around a prestigious university professor in linguistics who is diagnosed with Alzheimer's disease at age 50. I fully identified with the character.

Alice talks about the shame of having the disease. It is something I've given a lot of thought too. Why can people say they have a disease such as diabetes or hypertension without feeling that they are sharing some of their intimacy and why isn't it the same with a neurodegenerative disease? I imagine it must be tremendously hard to communicate that you have cancer, but I don't think it embarrasses you. Why do I not want people to know about my disease? I go back to what I said at the beginning. I guess it is because of the humiliating situations triggered by physical symptoms. As for now, no one notices my symptoms, I can choose not to tell. Not to be watched, not to get stressed when I feel people watching me, not to feel less than anyone else.

Alice also says that before the onset of the disease symptoms, intelligence defined her. And that was one of the first things I felt. It threatened everything I thought defined me. The goals I had set for myself had become unachievable or no longer made sense. What used to be the backbone of my life turned out to be no longer important for me.

There are races I've already abandoned because I know I will not make it. One day I told my therapist in tears: «I feel like I failed». The challenge is to be born in another state. To review what defines me. To ask myself, what are my goals now and how do I want to achieve them? So many times in my life I have said: «If I want this not to bother me, I would have to be born again». This is my chance. When I saw the book *Reinventing Yourself* in a bookstore, I didn't hesitate to purchase it. I didn't know who had written it nor had I read reviews of the book, but I imagined that some of its contents would help me. I still can't finish reading it, I'm having a hard time concentrating.

One day I was invited to choose a tarot card. As I turned it over, I came across the Tower. I shuddered as I looked at the image of a burning tower struck by lightning and people jumping out of it. And when I read the meaning, I felt tears pouring from a deep place within me.

When this card appears we may have felt the earth sinking beneath our feet. This card represents the power of fire, consuming and purifying, which destroys and sweeps out the old. Suddenly, a higher event breaks the material, psychological and moral structures that no longer work, leaving only the essential foundations on which it will be rebuilt. The Tower of the ego staggers to its foundations. Everything we try to keep is destroyed and the supposed security of the past is irrevocably shaken. It demands a realization that everything that happens in life comes from eternal love to itself. Relief automatically follows trauma. Behind the pain and anguish produced by a collapse, life shines as a promise of new options, because life won't stop. How sad will the experience be? If we acknowledge that the rupture happened because it was necessary to «embrace» the change or at least find something positive about it, it will make it less traumatic. The Tower invites you to learn the lesson and get over it. To overcome the Tower means to overcome the fall, rupture or disarray with an elevation of mind and spirit. Prepare yourself for renewal, be open to a new awareness that will set you free from old patterns.

Everything shows me that the path is in renewal. It is impossible not to see the signs. I am convinced that this explains the irresistible attraction I have for trimming the vines. One day I stopped to look at the vines I had planted twenty years ago along dozens of meters of boundary walls. I didn't like what they had become. Their branches were already trunks accumulating dust, snails, insects, dry leaves, and much more. They surpassed the walls and invaded the neighbors' houses. They even climbed a utility pole that seemed to have become a tree.

Suddenly I felt like I wanted to tear all the old branches off the walls and leave only the roots to force them to sprout new branches and leaves. Armed with small pruning scissors, a blunt saw, and a screwdriver, I undertook the task, and I couldn't stop. I spent several hours a day for months until the sun went down. Shortly after that, not even the sunset represented a limit to the task, since my brother-in-law gave me a miner's flashlight in a secret friend game.

One day, my husband told me he was worried about this activity and asked me to discuss it with my therapist. But I told him it had a meaning for me and that someday I would write about it. It fascinates me to see how I can pull off the old branches until I reach the core of the plant. I am impressed by how quickly they bloom, even though I have not reached the purest branches. And I thought how easy it is to get confused thinking there is a rebirth, even though the old cysts are still there under the new sprouts. But what I want to see is the rebirth from the first branches. I don't want them to remain hidden behind others that have imprisoned them for years. My husband says that the vines shake when they see me, and I finish the sentence to myself: «...to the beat of the tarot».

Tearing up a vine forces us to observe many things: what branch is there, no matter how fine it may seem, that does not allow others to peel off the wall. It impresses me to see how two branches join and form a new one, losing their individuality. It fascinates me to clean all the dust that has been accumulating for years between these branches and to see again the original color of the leaves. I am especially fascinated to allow them to grow back from their essence, liberated from what did not allow them to grow freely.

I promised several times to my family I would finish the task, but I did not keep my word. The day came when I gave it up. The truth is that I had to quit doing it because some ants bit me and I suffered from a terrible skin allergy for ten days... so terrible that I couldn't even get dressed. Now I water the vines often and moisten the walls to help them climb back. I know that I have to guide them and take care of them so they don't become entrenched again, so they always have fresh branches. The first thing I do early in the morning is to go out to the garden and I watch them sprouting with joy. They show me day by day in the dawn's silence that it is possible to rebirth.

One interpretation of the Tower card ended with this affirmation of one's power to make and remake oneself, that could not be more appropriate and tailored to what I've been feeling:

Opportunities emerge from crises. The terrain is fertile for new beginnings. I open myself to a necessary renewal, to a radical change, which can precipitate. I am alert to the movement that destroys the obsolete and I take responsibility for my destiny. I don't fight against new circumstances, nor do I deny reality. I admit it and decide the way forward: harmonious, healthy, and progressive.

That's why I stiffened at finding the poem I started these pages with. It includes so many words and similar concepts or the same as those I have chosen to transcribe my experiences: walls, ballasts, protection, rubble, fears, security, collapse, challenge... I knew that it came to me with a meaning.

I feel that I have already begun on the marked path. And in that path I feel so much better about myself, with more harmony. I am less dissatisfied with everything, more tolerant, and I don't get mad when things don't work out the way I planned. I'm surprised by the drama that people create for minor issues. I can help them see it. I value other things. I can help unravel misunderstandings between people, mediating, and softening. My mother said to me: «Now you are a nicer person», and I feel that way. I came to question if health is the complete state of bio-psycho-social well-being, maybe I was sicker before I had Parkinson's…

From *fighting against* to *living with* the disease

March 2015

I am often told that my fight against the disease is admirable and courageous, but I no longer feel at war. Parkinson's disease doesn't kill you, you don't have to fight it to keep living. Many times I think it must be terrible to have to battle day by day against something inside of you. I imagine it must feel like you're poisoned and that fighting increases the poison.

When I managed to make the change, I started to see everything differently. I assumed that the disease will be with me for the rest of my life and that it is part of me. It is as much a part of me as any other part of my body. There is no point in denying it, resisting it, but the great lesson is in finding how to live with it. And to face it in that context. Furthermore, it is necessary to establish codes of coexistence and to recognize when these have been broken.

My neurologist told me the first day that I had to become familiar with the disease. At that moment I didn't fully comprehend. Then I understood that knowing it and learning to live with it meant accepting it as a companion. It meant knowing what's good for you and what's not and acting accordingly. Re-learn how long things take now. Expect worsening symptoms. Look for solutions for what's complicated for you. And do everything you can to slow their pace. Because the disease will continue to advance, though no one can expect exactly what its evolution will be in every case. And as it is not possible to know, the best approach is to live the present day by day. Looking at it that way, it's not so complicated.

I also don't expect or feel like anyone should admire me for my process. While you are going through this process, the last thing on your mind is to seek admiration from others! I thought of how to better explain it. Imagine you're going on vacation on an airplane. A trip you planned to your preference, for which you chose your travel companions, the places you wanted to know, the hotels you'd like to stay in. Everything seemed under control and sounded perfect. Suddenly, the emergency door opens and you fall in the middle of the ocean. The water is freezing. You go into shock. You don't know on which side the land is closer to you. You are alone with only what you carried on with you: strength, calm, knowing how to swim, optimism; you will surely find something. You appeal to what is useful to you. There is no time to build up new skills. You do what you can, what comes naturally, with the strengths and skills you have. Suddenly, a person appears in a lifeboat and he says: «How admirable, how brave, what a fighter!». Surely, in that situation, the last thing you care about is another person's admiration. Surely, what you would like to say to this person is: «Brave? I'm slapping around, trying to keep myself from drowning. I'm only doing what I can to survive. I don't care if you admire me, what I need is your help. I need you to give me a hand to get out of the water. I need a blanket so I don't freeze to death. I need you to tell me I can get out alive, that you trust me, that you will be there for whatever I need».

A few days ago I had a family constellation session and had the opportunity to seek the meaning of the illness, which I have asked myself from the earliest days. It was the strongest, most incredible, and moving thing I have ever experienced in my entire life. I found the answer I was looking for, but where I least expected it. I also found the reason for that level of anguish that I have had for many years yet does not align with my life experiences.

The day after the constellation was a cool, gray autumn Sunday. I felt like going for a swim after years of not doing so. And with only the company of warm water and the resonance of my thoughts I swam 30 laps until I stopped when I saw that it was getting late for lunch.

I swam and realized that I was veering to the left; as I swam faster my arm on that side was like an oar that wanted to make a turn. And as I swam, I tried to go over what I had experienced the day before. It moved me tremendously. I know I couldn't record everything that happened. I know I can't nor should I pass the experience on.

I thought about how much I have used in this book words or expressions such as «without guilt», «imprisoned», «ties»... Even when someone comments on my new haircut, very short, I answer: «I feel released». At some point I was aware of the colossal weight I was enduring.

Now the disease has a face for me. The face of a calm man who looks me in the eye and says: «I am here for you». I see that from now on we will be together, but it's not a matter of a fight; it's a matter of gratitude. And of coexistence.

And as I swam and swam, I remembered how my father appeared in the scene. He didn't have a representative in the constellation. However, when we were finishing the coordinator looked at me and said: «You can do what you're feeling». Then I went to that man who represented Parkinson's and hugged him, and I realized that I was hugging my father. I can't explain it, but I know that my body understood it. I thought then, on a level that I cannot understand, my father was protecting and releasing me of a tremendous weight I carried. And I felt, as the water discreetly carried away my tears, that that would be the greatest act of love my father could have ever had towards me. I'll never know, but I like to imagine and sense that this experience reconciled me with him.

The day I turned 50

February 2016

The day I turned 50, I did face it. Not only did I face it, but I celebrated it in a big way. I had been feeling like celebrating and being grateful for some time.

I did the guest list thinking about who I wanted to join me that day and not who I had to invite. That set up an unique group of 80 people.

I phoned an old friend to help me with the centerpieces. I had been thinking about it for quite some time. I wanted them to have some meaning for me. I especially wanted my garden to be present at my party: in it, I had found an inexhaustible source of therapy.

From it I got the fruits of the Sweetgum, branches of Abelia, Palm leaves, flowers of Lily of the Nile plants that a friend gave me as a present, and also Hydrangeas. From a reunion a few days back with another friend from my childhood I brought as souvenir pebbles, Oak acorns, and Guadua. I collected fruits of gum trees that remind me of Rivera Street, the one I used to take to school on my bike, and I bought slices of pine to put underneath the centerpieces reminding me of the scent on the street where I lived until I got married. I also asked her to put sand on them, the one I walk and run on often in the early mornings and the one that frees me from the stiffness of my legs.

And finally came the last wish: that every arrangement had to be different, for that which I try to reaffirm, there's also beauty in imperfection.

The chosen date was a Friday in February, before Carnival week. That was not a reason for absences since the guests took incredible measures to be there, like rescheduling the dates of chemotherapy, moving the time of the dialysis forward, postponing their flights, or coming back early from the beach.

The night was spectacular; the temperature was ideal, the energy that reigned was perfect, and I felt that people were in sync with me. My family composed and sang a song for me that made me cry out laughing, and my sister practiced for months to present three pieces of tango. And then we danced for hours. Sometimes I think I don't know if I will have the will to keep on celebrating, or how much time I'll be able to dance, but I don't care. I have really incorporated the concept of the now or never.

A few years ago, I wouldn't have imagined that I would celebrate my 50th birthday. My mom said that quickly when she announced the song. I got her point perfectly because it was a shared feeling. But the moment came, and I had the will to celebrate, and overall to be grateful.

I was also feeling like saying something, but also anxious about it. I thought about writing what I wanted to say to the guests and putting it next to a board with pictures over the number 50 that I had prepared with my daughters. But I didn't have the time or couldn't. But when I blew out the candles and someone passed me the microphone, I took the plunge... I started and got emotional, and almost didn't continue, but one friend shouted: «Come on, Flor, you can do it!», and that was enough for me not to quit.

I don't remember living a night as intensely as this one. I was feeling full and overjoyed. The incredible thing is that the stone-carved guests of stiffness, fatigue, dysphonia, or difficulty to talk did not appear at all that evening, surely inhibited by so much love and good energy.

Survival mode and energy-saving mode

I think in this first stage I could say that I spent one year in survival mode and two in energy-saving mode.

It is absolutely revealing. I believe that all people should have the opportunity to experience it.

When you're in survival mode, you're just doing that, surviving. Best you can. Everything else is meaningless. Then, one magically emerges from the survival mode and switches to energy-saving mode. That means something like: «Very well, you survived, now you have to see how you will manage to move on». You preserve the energy for the important things. There is no place for commitments, compliments or to please others. Their opinions are irrelevant.

It's interesting, because when life puts you in these modes, your true essence emerges, permission to be oneself, the release of burdens, the authentic self…

It was not until now that I'm getting out of energy-saving mode, that I consider myself ready to return to the world of Mafalda, but unfortunately there are no substitutes in this life.

PART II

«Going past fears to discover the wonders of something different»

From May to August 2017

I heard it from Antonia — a blind woman — and it impacted me. I asked her if I could borrow it for something I was writing. The idea of «going past fears» caught me. And the idea of discovering what is on the other side: something different, unknown, opportunities? Would it be possible to find something across that would positively surprise me? I went past fears. But I did it while I struggled to flee from the anxiety, which, like a furious hurricane, was dragging me at 200 miles per hour. I managed to go to the other shore and to begin to see the half-full glass. It surprised me when I started to tick what was in it. There was much more in that list than I could have imagined.

Molotov cocktail

May 2017

I haven't written in over a year. I was getting intimate with anxiety. I can properly say that I am familiar with it up close. I can say that I know what it's like to *burst from anxiety*.

The year 2016 came loaded with potent emotions. I turned 50. My youngest daughter had partial facial paralysis and the oldest one went on an eight-month trip around the world. My aunt, my father-in-law, and my mother's husband passed away. All three losses had connotations that made them particularly tough or heartbreaking. At work, we changed our institutional dependence and moved to another office. My boss at the time took another job, and another director was named in her place. I traveled to Turkey to meet my daughter, and the occasion overlapped with the attempted coup d'état. The terrorist attacks in Europe were hot at our heels. I stepped away from two friends because of issues I did not have the strength to face. If intense emotions and stress are to Parkinson's the same as kryptonite is to Superman, I had more kryptonite in one year than I could have endured over a decade.

At the same time, my right leg ached so badly that I couldn't help limping and it bothered me to sleep.

The pain diminished while running, so I walked to the *rambla* and then tried to run through the sand. But afterward the pain returned even stronger, so I gave in to the temptation of resting. The pain would come even after practicing tai-chi.

My weak balance crumbled. Turning down the intensity and frequency of physical activity was disastrous. Anxiety and depression escalated, and I entered a circle from which I could not escape. But when all this was compounded by an incompatible combination of medication and homeopathy, I felt like I had drunk a Molotov cocktail.

I know that anxiety is often present among people with Parkinson's disease. It may originate from the stress provoked by the diagnosis or may be directly related to the neurochemical changes in the brain. Medication might also contribute. Reading the lengthy list of its side effects scares me. And compared to hallucinations, compulsive behaviors like gambling or sex, or falling asleep suddenly, among dozens of other possibilities, anxiety sounds like nonsense. But it can be both exasperating and exhausting for the one who experiences it.

I knew what it meant being unable to rest for months. I was incapable to lay back and do nothing, neither watch a movie nor read a book. I absolutely couldn't. Actually, I needed to do over one thing at a time. I think that's the reason I write in my head while I do my exercises... because it's the only other thing I can do while I'm moving!

Anxiety prompted me to do unusual, out of place or inappropriate things, such as buying a stool on Facebook while undergoing physiotherapy on a stretcher, interrupting people when they were talking or playing on the phone in front of a guest. In the eagerness to be active, and because of the inability to keep from doing things even for a scant time, I wouldn't even watch the evening news on TV. One day I arrived at the tai-chi class and from the conversations I overheard, I realized that Donald Trump had won the elections the day before. I must have been the only person on earth not following the news. I must have been focused on some inventions in my creativity corner.

Later on, I also felt the effects of anxiety when I traveled as a passenger in a car. Sometimes I would open the door shaking. On one occasion, I couldn't resist getting out of the car when my husband intended to cross a busy avenue.

With time, the anxiety became stronger and became insufferable. One day I felt it had crossed the threshold of what I could resist, and I checked the medications I was taking. I discovered that there was Hypericum (or St. John's wort) in the latest homeopathic preparations. I knew that there was a dangerous side effect while taking medication prescribed by my neurologist. But I kept reading facts and found that it also exacerbated the anxiety side effect of another prescription given by the psychiatrist. I immediately stopped homeopathy drops and halted the burst of anxiety. But I went a step further and took the risk without consulting my psychiatrist and stopped taking the pills which caused anxiety. When I woke up the next day, I felt a marvelous sensation of freedom and an extreme pressure lifted.

Anyway, the anxiety was still present, but it didn't overwhelm me. I also had a level of apathy that kept me from taking the steps I knew I needed to undergo to feel better. It's hard to explain that apathy can coexist with anxiety, but it does. I couldn't figure out how to get out of that situation. I kept telling myself that if I had a little more energy, I could overcome the barriers. I felt stuck.

Boisterous ideas
bustle in my brain and
burst as they reach the boiling point

Anxiety began right after the diagnosis. I would wake up and jump out of bed. Lingering wasn't by any means an option to consider. My husband told me one day: «I didn't see you back in bed in the morning». My head did not stop generating ideas for me to accomplish or home modification to contract.

In the last year I hand-polished the wooden floor on the ground floor, I disassembled all the locks to scrap the varnish; I unscrewed the bathroom faucets to remove the enamel. I hand-picked the weeds out of the garden with such dedication, as if I was preparing to receive an inspection for an ISO 9000 accreditation. I had the floor of the upper level changed, and a few months later I had the entire house painted. Every corner I should say, down to the bottom of the closets, which forced me to empty them. Then I changed the coating of the staircase. I reached level 1000 in the Candy Crush game.

I made a list of 44 projects ranging from sanding and painting shelves to upholstering a stool, or making a 99 square patchwork quilt. My husband said that they were pharaonic projects because they all had some particularity that made them especially challenging: the size, the level of difficulty, the seemingly impossible condition of the task.

I would get the materials as I came up with ideas, but not as I accomplished previous projects. I needed to be certain that if I had the opportunity to undertake any of these initiatives, I would have all the resources. Near my office, there is a fabric sale house that has snippets in boxes and out of stock upholstery. Now and then, or every so often, I go for a walk to see what's there. And there's always an old man whom I think trembles when he sees me arrive because he knows that I will stir things around for a long time, I take a long time deciding, and I also expect him to give me a special price on what is already a bargain! The question is always the same: «What are you looking for, madam? And the answer is always the same: «Nothing special, I'm just looking». But I almost always buy something, to have... in case the opportunity arises.

I also made sure I had ideas to run according to tiredness, weather, or sunlight. Whoever has never experienced this may not understand the dimension of what I have just written. A machiavellian mechanism that guaranteed that there would never be an excuse to rest. There was no: «It's raining today and I can't paint», or «I'm tired enough to sand», or «with artificial light, I find it hard to sew with black thread, so I will watch a movie». I always had choices of things to do and all the materials.

One day I told my younger brother about my unbelievable list, and he told me: «You have a project for each weekend, from now until the end of the year». That was an intelligent guess. But I started each day aiming to finish three or four, but I could barely complete half of the endeavors because of the slowness of my hands and the fatigue?

And in each of these projects, there was a special delight in making use of the resources I found around the house, reusing objects and materials classified as obsolete, or in assigning them new and important functionality. I think what attracts me most about this exercise is that it mocks what I'm trying to do to myself: identify my resources, appeal to what I already had, rediscover myself, build a new identity based on what already existed. But I also suspect that an in-depth need to embrace the present time is dying this compelling desire of realizing all kinds of projects; an urge not to waste a single minute *now that I can do it.*

Creativity & Perfectionism Inc.: Working for Parkinson's

When I got my Master's degree in Nutrition, three years prior to my Parkinson's diagnosis, my mother gave me a curious gift... a spectacular sewing machine. Let's just say it isn't a very conventional present for someone who gets an academic major degree. It took me several months to find the time to learn to use it, but sewing has been, in the last few years, one of my biggest hide-outs.

Yes, sewing... I spend endless hours in each project, endless hours that vanish at the speed of light, but I show my finished projects as trophies, with more pride than the books I published or the outstanding grades I got in an exam. My therapist says that my eyes shine when I tell her about my latest creation, and my husband confirms that this is so. And I tell, bursting with laughter, how I turned old and outdated items into new and unthinkable things.

Although it's sometimes a little frustrating, I love to sew, and it does me good. I've spent up to half an hour trying to thread a needle and twice I have called my husband for help, pouting. I've tried threaders, but they don't always work for me. I let creativity help me with my problems. I take out the sewing machine needle, thread it and place it back in. To sew by hand, I prick the needle in a needle holder and I thread it in that position.

I felt like creating a room in the house for me to give free rein to creativity. To do this, I sold all the furniture in my home office. That meant emptying two entire libraries while deciding that I didn't want to keep all those papers and books. I had nothing to envy the General Archives of the Nation. My colleagues didn't even bother to keep anything; they knew that I had everything classified and that I would also remember where everything was. I even had backup files in Wordstar... many people won't even know what I'm talking about.

The person who bought me the furniture, seeing the task I had in front of me with all those books and folders, said: «It makes me feel lazy!». I listened to her in surprise as I thought of how much time I hadn't felt lazy or pronounced that word. I threw it all away. I kept a handful of books. I even removed the professional title from the frame as I thought: «Why do I want to have this hanging in my house?».

I chose the color purple to decorate my new space. Then I found out it's the color of transmutation. I bought an old sewing machine base to make a work table. I could have chosen one that I would not have to restore, but I fell in love with the one that had six little adorable drawers, although it required many hours of sanding and painting. I made and sanded wooden boards and painted them to work as shelves. I bought some drawers in an auction and I wrapped the front of them with a cloth that I padded. I also wrapped boxes and folder holders and the cork billboard. The bin escaped neither. With a handmade belt, I made some shooters for a closet, so I transformed an ordinary piece of furniture into something unique and eye-catching. The result is a space I love to be in. Just for me. My shelter. Where I sew and write as I look at the garden. Where I let my creativity fly. And doing so is an incomparable resource for me.

Creativity has also helped me to come up with solutions to everyday situations. While with a little more time I would say I can do just about anything, there are days or situations where a little help is very welcome. With wires of different thicknesses, I made myself some wire hooks to button shirts without help. I started using the term Parkinson Friendly. At first, I used it to refer to a selection of accessories I separated because they were very easy to wear. In the same way, I imagined some combinations of clothes that did not require a challenge and to which I could turn to when I have to change in the club or I am in a hurry at home.

But I also realized that I could let creativity help me with other difficulties I have. One of the most complicated situations I have to deal with daily is putting things in and taking things out of my handbag. And if it's full of obstacles, the challenge is tremendous.

I analyzed the conditions that a handbag would have to have to be Parkinson Friendly:

- It had to be a shoulder strap handbag to let my arms free.

- It couldn't be too big to lose things inside, or too small for everything to be tight, which makes it difficult to maneuver objects in its place. That is to say, I had to define with enough precision what I would carry in it daily.

- It should not have obstacles that exacerbate the difficulty to put in and take out. These are generated especially when there are objects left halfway through, such as those that emerge from open interior pockets, pencils or other objects that block the way, and so on.

- It must have a lot of direct and individual access, easily identifiable for what one has to find quickly: the phone and the keys. For the latter, I thought the best thing would be to hold them to a ribbon, so they don't fall at the worst moment. These direct accesses had to have a zipper that was both easy to operate and safe.

- It should be easy to open and close, possibly magnets were the best solution.

- A small, easily accessible exterior pocket to separate the money and cards I would need in the next destination, so I don't have to be opening the purse and wallet while everyone waits.

- A large pocket to tip over everything you get back at the cash register of a store where one has to store quickly everything while the rest of the customers wait impatiently. Place the bills orderly in the wallet, the coins in their compartment, do the same with the customer card and the receipt, when at the same time the cashier gives you the bag with the purchase... it is too much to ask!

- Few internal pockets. To be more precise: two. With one extra detail: each one should have a zipper of a different color, because symmetries upset me and my poor memory doesn't help, and I never remember which side each thing is on.

It took me over a year to finish it, but I succeeded. The major difficulty wasn't the stiffness of my hands but deciding how to do it. It looked spectacular and when I finished it I felt so proud that I held it as a medal of honor. When I reflect on this feeling, which seems exaggerated compared to other achievements that I have accomplished throughout my life, I think I know where it comes from: it is proof that you can.

Some people tell me I should do things to sell, to which I reply that if I were to charge for the hours that each thing takes me, nobody would buy me anything.

Later I found a piece of news that said that Parkinson's medication turned patients into artists, such as sculptors, painters, or writers. The fact that Parkinson's medication decreases inhibitions could explain this, enabling patients to accept their creativity.

In what corner of my brain did you hide, creativity? What suppressed you?

A *heavy* family tradition

There's a very *heavy* tradition in my family. The one who completes higher education receives upon graduating a massif bronze cube. The rest of the family engrave personalized messages in each of its 6 sides, which are as heavy as the very object that contains them.

The sides of the cube I received had the following verses. I understood so many things after reading the messages again...

To Florencia, Licensed. With pride, your family that adores you. Continue the example of your parents: inexhaustible legacy and treasure. You give much love and care; you can count on the same from us. Keep on being good, kind, and hardworking. There is happiness in an industrious life. Preserve your strength and enthusiasm; we will continue to savor your stories. Take from life its ineffable beauty and make of each day a memorable banquet.

I now, irreverently, use it to hold the fabrics I'm measuring and cutting because there's no chance that they will move under that solid piece.

Everyone, except my mother, had their cube. I wanted her to have her own, so I made it by myself. But this cube it's not made of bronze, it's a tissue box. It also has its six sides engraved, but with messages of love, of recognition and gratitude. Because I realize counting on my mother's unconditional love was crucial to my process. I knew that she would still love me no matter what version of me came up. So I ignored the stiffness of my hands and lined each side with an allusive design using the patchwork technique.

The messages I put on the four end sides the end sides were:

«Ph.D. as an unconditional companion of any proposed program... and so many afternoons of sewing. Thank you, Mommy!». I decorated this side with pieces of the last things we sewed together.

«Dad's love for art is also in you, me, and this cube». To represent it, I made a kind of construction out of ties that had belonged to my father.

«Mother always present, both in my birth and in my rebirth at the 50s. You're unique, Mommy!». I lined this side with the fabric of the dress that I wore on my 50th birthday and that my mother helped me fit.

«Crowned as the queen of recycling... I follow your steps, Mommy!». I made this side up of ribbons, gallons, and festoons of unthinkable origins. The most incredible thing is that I could recall where each one came from!

On its upper side is a piece of cloth with which my mother wrapped the bassinet used by my daughters: «To my adored mother, *licensed honorary cause* as super mommy». She deserves it: she was my mother twice. As present at my birth as in my rebirth at the 50s, when the diagnosis of Parkinson's disease threatened everything that gave me security. Everything but my mother's love.

When the tic-toc
doesn't run the same for everyone

I live with the feeling that the clock tics faster for me. I can't believe every time I look at it.

Several times I was tempted to measure the time each task takes me, to understand why I'm never on time. Because it's not just a bit more. It's a lot more. I am not exaggerating if I say that it is double or triple time, depending on the complexity of the task. But this applies to every micro-movement I make. For example, having a latte means opening the refrigerator, taking the milk, choosing a cup, pouring the milk, opening the microwave, putting the cup inside, closing the oven. Opening the oven, adding the coffee, previously having prayed that whoever passed through the kitchen before did not drink it. And the list goes on: opening the sweetener lid, pouring a few drops, a few!, closing the lid, putting it in place, taking out a spoon, stirring the coffee with milk, washing the spoon... All these tasks finished just to begin the next challenge: bringing the cup to the mouth and swallowing. And when it's time to eat and get dressed, you do millions of micro-movements, with astonishing slowness.

And since Parkinson's disease slows down the start and execution of voluntary movements, many beginnings mean many delays.

But the worst of it is that the more you try to hurry, the more difficult it is to execute with success the movement.

My family has already learned that the most counterproductive thing they can do is to rush me. They have banished from their lexicon the questions: «How long will you take?» or the classic: «Will you finish soon?».. Instead of pressuring me with those questions, they often appear asking if I need help.

As a child, a friend of mine told me that her grandmother used to say: «I'm going slowly because I'm in a hurry». I always remember that. It's the best premise to apply.

To be overcomed
by a sugar packet

Few things intimidated me. In fact, the bigger the challenge, the more excited I became about it. I would face a crowded conference room, a demanding student group, or an insidious journalist without fear. I could have finished my master's thesis easily, but I chose the hard way. The one that challenged me enough: a new topic that forced me to study many hours and several research questions that could have been addressed by at least three master's students.

My new adversaries are seemingly harmless and insignificant objects. It takes a gigantic wave of humility to declare oneself overcomed by a sugar packet that resists being opened or by the eye of a needle that refuses to let the thread pass. Or to accept my daughter's offer to cut the meat for me or my co-workers' empathy to sit at my computer keyboard for me to dictate to them when they see that we will not finish the task in time, as they say to me: «This way we go faster». Or at least we narrow the gap between the speed of my ideas and that of my hands. Sometimes I think rather than just a wave of humility, I had to drown in it.

I also needed humility when the physiotherapist taught me how to walk to avoid the pain in my legs. I came into the office and told my team: «Today I learned to walk like a baby». This starting over is a serious business.

Getting rid
of the superwoman cape

I used to be a model girl. An outstanding student at school; I took piano, cooking, theatre, and English lessons; attended a craft workshop and learned to sew with my mother. As a teenager, I dared to rebel a little, but always taking care not to transgress the margins allowed by the «what will they say».

As an adult, I played at being the superwoman. I fulfilled my roles as a woman, mother, wife, and worker trying to get an «A» in each dimension. Several times I came across comments such as «Everything that Florencia does, she does it well». And every time they kept resonating in my head. Sometimes the comment involved an acknowledgment, but other times was loaded with a hint of annoyance. The truth is that it happened as much in the work environment as in the family and friends' circles. Although on the one hand, I liked to listen to them, I was always thinking and feeling that this was a topic to touch in my therapy.

It wasn't until I turned into my 40s I began to give my husband some space, when I took a master's degree and came home at 10:00 p.m. several days a week. When I arrived, I saw through the dining room curtain the silhouettes of my husband and daughters around the table. Everything had gone smoothly and they had dined in harmony. I admit that acknowledging that I was not so essential bothered me a little. Surrendering the power was not total from the beginning; I left everything planned and wrote the menu for each day. This situation allowed me to see that it is oneself who does not want or let others occupy certain spaces that give security and power.

Later on, I realized that if I wanted to get out of that role I had to give up the real space. Biting my tongue if the brand of oil that my husband bought was not the one I would have chosen, or happily eating the unbalanced menu that he prepared making no criticism, waiting for the right moment to make the suggestions for future occasions.

I'm not sure why, but with the diagnosis, I started to reject taking care of the kitchen and household chores, and I let my husband take care of the shopping, the kitchen, our daughters, and absolutely everything. Not everything, actually. My husband abandoned the household repairs, which I now practically do on my own. He developed his culinary skills while I learned to use the drill. Sometimes I think this rejection may have had to do with the desperate need to feel cared for, with the impossibility of assuming my maternal and nurturing role. When I see my husband doing the housework, I feel bad, but I justify myself by thinking the first 25 years of marriage I was the one who did most of it.

Anything that breaks or needs maintenance is presented to me as a challenge and I don't stop until I solve it. In general, I do it. I think that behind this is again the search for: «I can». The family, surprised to see these skills, brings me the impossible cases for me to solve. I have repaired a sculpture by placing an inner screw like a surgeon; I rebuilt an accessory for the bathroom that had been reduced to shards like a crushed cookie; I repaired a mill that had a musical box and that the family had decided to take to a watch repair shop.

When the symptoms of Parkinson's start, you realize that you lost your career as a superwoman and that you're not interested in running the race either. I noticed that some people find it useful to have a superwoman nearby. They must find another superfriend or get by on their own.

Bye-bye, superwoman cape! What a relief not to have to wear you anymore! And I don't give you away because no woman deserves you. In Eduardo Galeano's words, perfection is «the boring privilege of the gods». I am human and I also have Parkinson's.

Anyway, I think I still have a lot to work in this field. I was thinking about this when one member of my team, the last to join, when looking at a picture of me in a hot-air balloon, asked me if I was handling it...

A lab in the Office

My work and professional performance always occupied a place of hierarchy in my life. Perhaps I should say that it disputed the first place with the family in my ranking of priorities. My work life was dementia. I accepted any work proposal I received, and I spent all day working. I worked as a consultant, as a professor, and frequently coordinated projects for an international organization. At one point I realized that I had seven bosses.

With the diagnosis, I thought my professional career and my chances of holding positions of responsibility were vanishing. I was working as a consultant on an early childhood project in a government office and I coordinated an important area. I also coordinated a thematic area in a master's degree at a private university. I taught and tutored theses in various undergraduate and graduate programs in the country and remotely. To be honest, the diagnosis found me at the peak of my professional life. Sitting in a corner office overlooking the sea in the Presidency of the Republic, at the top professional position. Symbolically, I could not be higher.

I didn't need much analysis to realize that I couldn't keep up with that work pace. To make room for my self-care activities, to get less stressed out, and not to exhaust myself so much. One by one, I thoroughly analyzed each of my jobs to decide which one to keep and which one to give up. This was the beginning of a painful path of resignations. I started by giving up those jobs that gave me less satisfaction. I continued for those who brought me less income and, lastly, for the one that gave me more academic prestige and I liked it better but entailed me to dedicate a significant part of my weekends.

The decisions were rational to me, but they hurt me so much. I had conquered each of those spaces by merit and with a lot of effort. I had dedicated several years of my life to them and I was always trying to go one step ahead.

One day, after having completed my last resignation, I went to visit my noble companion throughout the years, on this path and adventure called work. Long before the diagnosis, she had already noticed that something was wrong with me. Actually, she was the only one who perceived it. She had been out of the country for a year and on her return, she saw me changed. She worriedly called my husband, saying that I seemed slower in my movements. But my husband replied that he noticed nothing wrong with me and erased this conversation from his memory. I know the tremendous impact that the news of my diagnosis had on her. And although now we do not work side by side as before, she has been as present in this stretch of my path as when we shared eternal days of work. That day, we talked at length about an academic project that we founded together, but that at the time was difficult to sustain from various points of view. However, she continued to defend it with cloak and sword. When we were saying goodbye, separated by the elevator door, I said: «You're fighting windmills». Only that. She looked at me with wide eyes. The next day she presented her letter of resignation. She reminds me of that and is over and over thankful. She left me thinking I must be very convincing and I have to be very careful with the words I say.

I think for the first time in my life I stayed with just one job, consulting. When I remember the first post-diagnosis times, I really don't understand how I kept on working. Where did I get the strength if I was in shock? If my head was at the same time trying to answer the most existential questions.

The change of government was approaching and with it the conceived changes in the positions of responsibility. You could see that everyone was trying to accommodate themselves as best they could, but I felt that I was out of the ring and I didn't make any movement. However, my new boss proposed to me a new position which implied additional responsibilities and I took up the challenge. They gave me some allowances that let me better manage my time and take away my stress. But at the same time, they make me feel guilty…

One day I told my therapist how comfortable I felt in my office, in the sense of being able to talk and handle everything related to my disease, something I have not accomplished in any other circle. I believe that two key factors are frequency of encounter and proximity, to which I add a third: it is a unique group of people.

I lead a group of six people who, just by seeing me arrive, already know if I exercised in the morning. One day, when one of them saw me writing, she said to me: «It is obvious that today you went out on a run». On another occasion, we had to make a collective video juggling. I don't think the consultant who drew up the instructions could have imagined the challenge it posed for me. But a member of my team solved the problem immediately. She said to me with total ease: «You, who have the most difficulty with your hands are the one who throws the balls to the rest». And so it was. And I was practically at the head of the video. Worthily.

They also have learned to identify fatigue better than others. I get exhausted when I coordinate a meeting, as well as when I perform tasks that require a lot of concentration. It seems as if the nervous system is shutting down, going into pause mode. Explaining this sensation to those who haven't experienced it is mission impossible, so I usually just say: «I am tired», despite it has nothing to do with physical tiredness. My co-workers have found a more appropriate description: «Cerruti has turned off». They also talk about the «cheeks operation» to encourage me to eat when I'm too skinny. Only to them have I confessed with laughter how furious I become when I'm hungry and I'm still trying to put the first bite in my mouth after having fought with the cutlery for endless minutes, while I see that the others are ready to ask for another dish. Only to them, besides my husband, I have accepted at some point the offer of help to stop struggling with cutlery. Only they, when they go out to look for food they will suggest to me: «Not that pie, it's very difficult to cut».

It's strange because I'm respected as a boss, they seek my opinion on everything they do, but at the same time, they know my limitations like no one else. They take care of me and protect me. It is my team that helps me plan my days so I have time for physical activity, because it doesn't go unnoticed by them that

I'm someone else when I do exercise, and that my ideas flow differently and I can transmit them clearly. They tell me things like: «Healthy time to leave, Cerruti», or «I remind you what you say to me; don't wait to feel bad, stop in time».

It's just that they've seen me get exhausted. One day they told me they had learned to identify the signs that showed that I was exhausted. I asked intrigued what they were. The answer was: «Your face, Flor». I am aware of the stiffness that appears and transforms my expression. Recently I started doing facial mimic exercises to help loosen muscles. I must look crazy, I do them while I drive, while I walk through the corridors of work. Also, when I see my mental performance slowing down, I go out and take a brisk walk a few blocks away. And when I can't stop the fatigue in time, I sit in a couch and wait a few minutes for the nervous system to recover.

My therapist said: «You have a lab in your office». That lab shows me that what I want is possible. What I still don't know is how to bring other situations to that level. It's clear to me that the dialogue: «Do you know I have Parkinson's?», «Oh, I didn't know, can I help you with something?», is just a fantasy. One can be prepared to talk about it (or almost), but it does not imply that others can receive it.

It took me a while to realize that my process had also been hard for my team. On the one hand, because the news affected them, but also because, acting with immense nobility, they filter problems from me, or they would step in situations I had not resolved, adapting to my changing moods, energy, and performance. One day I said to one of them: «I feel that it's not fair for you». And she answered with blurred eyes: «That is not fair for us, Flor?… and for you?».

I told my team that I would soon move on to a new stage of treatment, incorporating levodopa and that the doctor said I would be back to my old self. He was reluctant to move on to this new phase until I told him I didn't know how much longer I could keep up the pace of work because of the fatigue. I saw their faces of horror when they said: «The one from before? Every day will be like Mondays?». We laughed together, but we all knew that the old me of before is gone.

On the other side of fear...
What good did Parkinson's bring me?

There's no doubt in my mind that getting here meant facing the greatest challenge life has ever put in front of me. I always liked challenges. I remember my diagnosis happened on a Friday and I told my boss about it over the weekend. First thing Monday morning she was in my office. When she asked how I was doing, my answer was: «It's a challenge and I like challenges».

I didn't measure the true magnitude of the challenge. The multitude of edges that I would have to deal with. How difficult it would be for me. The temptation to throw everything overboard that would appear in over one opportunity.

But I review many paragraphs I have written along these pages and with no doubt, there were many wins. I can see it from the first pages. In aspects I wanted to change and that I wouldn't let myself, but also in the discovery of other aspects of my personality that were not accessible and in learning so much, but so much, from life itself. Some wins were collateral; they were brought about as I dared to do so deep insight.

It allowed me to take more care of myself without feeling guilty, to work less, to say no to job offers and to say no to more things, to stop doing things to please other people, to stay more at home, to be more human and not so perfect, to develop other facets of my personality and to do other activities that I like, as writing, for example, or giving free rein to creativity or dedicate hours to gardening.

It gave me a huge bath of humbleness that makes me more accessible to others. I had to learn to accept that I'm vulnerable and I need help. It was very difficult for me, more than anyone could imagine, especially when my daughters or my co-workers were involved. But I recognize that now a smaller distance separates me from the others, which allows me to connect with people in a new and enjoyable way.

It gave me peace, as I feel that I am achieving greater inner harmony, not being always dissatisfied with everything, and being more and more tolerant, understanding that the level of anguish that I felt over me was not mine, when I felt that I had reconciled with my father, who left 23 years ago and left things due to close.

It taught me how to live day by day. As the poem *Don't give up* says: Because this is the time and the best moment...». It became my header poem.

It allowed me to generate new ties: with vulnerable people as I now feel I can connect with their pain; with deep people interested in deep dialogues; with my body by being more connected with it and by learning how to hear it. Sometimes I feel like I can sniff out others´ fear, even though I've lost much of my sense of smell.

It gave me some privileges and a lot of pampering from the people who love me. My husband got his passport for the first time and we started to travel. So far he had been stubborn and we traveled very little and as far as his identity card would allow us. I stopped arguing for this reason and I quenched my thirst for travel with my childhood friends or in business trips. Besides, very generous invitations came from my mother and siblings to escape the cold in the winter. My family tells me, happy as well, that now I let them hug me...

It taught me what I would never have learned. I found myself enrolled in many, intensive, and difficult courses in life. Of the ones I like and those with the best method: «learning by doing».

I also gained multiple resources and for life skills which I find myself sharing and spreading from time to time. And I discovered that I feel more fulfilled than in any other circumstance when, based on my knowledge, I feel that I can help someone.

It gave me the legitimacy and authority to make some statements, to make some suggestions. People have told me: «I needed to talk to you», «I know you can understand me».

It made me a better version of myself. It was an invitation to rediscover myself, to start anew, to reflect on my mission in life. I have been told: «Now you are a nicer person», «I love this sweet version of you».

It freed me from wearing the heavy cape of a superwoman, which I was no longer interested in carrying. I walk so much lighter through life!

PART III

Out of fuel:
the pre-levodopa era

August 2017

New symptoms come and others accentuate. The disease becomes visible. I did not see it coming. I was not prepared enough. But much less did I expect that something still much more difficult would follow this stage: accepting others to treat me as a person with a disability. The pre- levodopa era represents the raw and face-to-face encounter with the disease. The daily management of symptoms, the adoption of aids or life adjustments to make life easier. The failed attempt in disguising what was happening to me. It was a time to learn to accept help from my daughters and my co-workers. Times in which each action, as insignificant as it might seem, involved such a tremendous effort that I thought about it several times before taking the challenge. But, above all things, were times of tough questions that involved monumental decisions.

Symptoms, nightmares, and panic attacks: talking about acceptances and adjustments

I had the chance to go through the acceptance process without having to explain what was happening to me, since the diagnosis occurred when the motor symptoms were just beginning. That was a relief! And it allowed me to solve one problem at a time — or at least not as many problems at once —, as I like to do.

But as in all neurodegenerative diseases, the symptoms advance, become visible and interfere with daily life, and the time to think about life adjustments comes, anyway.

I emphasize again that there is not one Parkinson's disease, but that there are as many versions as people who suffer from it. The rate at which the disease progresses is also variable. There is one word that properly sums up what one feels: uncertainty.

Like most people, at age 47 I knew nothing about Parkinson's. I believed it was a disease that affected only older people and caused them to tremble. Little by little, I gained knowledge about the disease by reading and informing myself, but above all as I found myself face to face with the symptoms. And I learned that tremor is only one of the motor symptoms and that it is not even always present in all patients. And that there is an extensive list of motor and non-motor symptoms. I wake up every day wondering what new symptom I will admonish.

Neurologists carry out tests and examinations to rule out other causes for the symptoms, but the diagnosis is essentially clinical since, as for now, no study confirms the disease. According to the International Parkinson and Movement Disorder Society (MDS-PD) the essential criterion is the presence of parkinsonism, which is defined as bradykinesia (slow movements), in combination with at least one between rest tremor and rigidity. This recent criterion has incorporated many non-motor manifestations, often dominating the clinical presentation of the disease, and requires the verification of the absence of other possible causes.

It is clear then, that the lack of tremor at rest does not mean that you can rule out the disease. It may be absent in one out of three people with Parkinson's.

Face to face with the symptoms

There are four major symptoms of the disease, all of them motor related. To be more illustrative, I will give examples of how I live with them, which does not mean that the same thing happens to other people with Parkinson's.

- **Slow movements**: both spontaneous and voluntary movements lose speed or are lost. When raising my two arms, the right one comes after the left. When walking, my right arm hardly sways. I take a long time to take the food to my mouth.

- **Stiffness**: the arms, legs, or other parts of the body lose flexibility. It was the first thing I noticed and for which I went to the doctor. The stiffness in my right hand did not allow me to write well. It is what difficulties me to handle silverware well, to thread a needle, to break a sachet of sugar, to button a necklace, to put the key in the lock, to make quick back and forth movements, such as washing my hair, to brush my teeth and thousands of others.

- **Tremor at rest:** An uncontrollable movement that affects the arms or legs when the person is at rest but disappears during a voluntary movement. It can also appear on the chin. I only feel it when I am experiencing very intense emotions. I especially felt it the day I read the email in which I was told that the story I had submitted to a literary contest had been among the top ten and that they would publish it along with the other nine finalists. I trembled uncontrollably.

- **Postural instability:** problems when standing or walking, or decreased balance and coordination. My gear changed, I take shorter steps, I hunch, sometimes my legs fail, but my balance is intact.

Besides these four major motor symptoms that are a condition for diagnosis, there are others that may also appear: decreased facial expressions; low voice volume; speech alterations such as becoming monotonous, low-pitched and intense, hoarse and choppy; increased salivation and drooling, as well as breathing difficulties. I have been told that my face changes in the late afternoon or when I am stressed. But they have also told me in the other sense. «It changed your face!»: one of my sons-in-law told me when I returned from vacations, as someone else told me when they saw me coming back from a brisk walk during a break from work.

I have noticed speech alterations. My voice is getting hoarse. I speak softer and softer and I have lost the ability to modulate my voice. It is very difficult to give a lecture or dictate a lesson without these audience attention catcher skills. These symptoms relate to the stiffness of the larynx that does not allow adequate closure of the vocal cords. And I must admit, although I am mortified to do so, that I don't drool, but saliva accumulates in the left side of my mouth. This appears to occur because swallowing frequency decreases.

To make matters worse, the disease does not end with motor problems, but there is a lengthy list of non-motor symptoms, which are also very frequent. And if no one attributes motor symptoms — except tremor — to Parkinson's, much less do they do so with non-motor symptoms. Because in addition, none of these symptoms are exclusive to the disease, but I would like to establish that only those who have experienced them from the condition of Parkinson's can understand me when I say that they feel different when the disease causes them.

On the one hand, there is a group of symptoms related **to mood and cognitive disorders:** depression, anxiety, decreased ability to perform various tasks or concentrate, slowed thinking, impulse control disorders, hallucinations, delusions and dementia. I would like to emphasize that the shock and impact of receiving the diagnosis can cause these issues, but also the chemical alterations in the brain can be blamed.

The challenge underlying the coordination of a work meeting could be a good example. The effort is so great that I become exhausted, just like the endeavor of trying to overcome the stiffness of my right hand when washing my hair. If I am interrupted, I lose track of what I was saying and that means... starting all over. Sometimes I give up. I try not to schedule two meetings in a row because I can't follow them, at least as I like to do. Concentrating is an odyssey, especially when it comes to tasks that require keeping the focus of attention for a long period.

However, I can instantly identify an error in a spreadsheet and detect the entire chain that led to that error. I have not lost my analytical capacity. Overcoming depression is not a simple job. There is always someone who tells me it is not convenient to take antidepressants since they «shadow the symptoms», and that it is best to see them in therapy. I would love to take the antidepressant I had to quit when the doctor prescribed me Parkinson's medication.

I dedicate several pages of this book to anxiety, but only as an extreme synthesis I will mention the only question my husband asked me when he learned of my meeting with other people with Parkinson's: «Do they have the same need to do things nonstop as you do?». I had only one hallucination, but it was a logical consequence of having taken two doses of the same medication too close to each other. And about impulse control, I could confess something: it wasn't just once that I went into a store to buy a dress and came out with four... As much as I try to explain that they were at a ridiculously cheap price, it never happened to me before.

We must also associate this with another symptom, which is the difficulty to make decisions. It feels as if a tidal wave is flooding your brain and not letting you decide. The interesting thing is that this entire group of symptoms improves after a good sleep or after exercising.

The disease usually affects sleep before motor symptoms manifest. There may be daytime sleepiness, nightmares, vivid dreams, insomnia, fragmented sleep, or restless leg syndrome. What I have had is the fragmented dream for many years. I wake up several times a night and crossing the threshold of six total hours of sleep is such a rare event that it deserves a celebration when it happens.

Another group of symptoms related to the connection between the brain and organs includes low blood pressure when standing, excessive sweating, seborrhea, sexual dysfunction, and urination disorders. I had seborrheic dermatitis and rosacea many years ago, and also episodes of excessive sweating. But here comes the other comment that one also frequently hears: «It's menopause, it happens to me too». And I do not deny the possibility. But why is the first reaction of people to look for another cause for your symptoms, or to tell you that the same thing happens to them? I do not doubt that they do it with the best intention, but it is not easy to hear it.

There are also digestive symptoms, such as difficulty swallowing, nausea, and constipation. I have noticed for a long time that I have to pay attention to the consumption of fiber and liquids to contribute to intestinal transit.

There are also sensory symptoms such as pain of unknown origin, tingling sensation, loss of smell, visual disturbances. I realize now that I can attribute to Parkinson's the loss of smell of some odors, such as that of perspiration or that of cinnamon. Or losing the ability to focus my vision.

Other symptoms include body changes, weight loss. I lost eleven pounds a while after the diagnosis. Then I partially recovered them.

Fatigue. If one had to select the most misunderstood and difficult to explain symptom, fatigue takes all the rewards. What is fatigue? How to explain it to someone who has never experienced it? I found a document that relates that patients with Parkinson's described fatigue as being: «tired, exhausted, without energy, unable to do anything, wanting to lie down all the time». It is not the same feeling you experience after a day of hard work. Parkinson's-related fatigue can be described as an unpleasant feeling of lack of energy, making it difficult to perform normal activities, both physical and mental.

About a third of patients with Parkinson's consider fatigue the most bothersome symptom, even compared to tremor, slowness, and trouble walking, freezing, and balance and speech problems. As common sense would show, people who experience fatigue do not enjoy life in the same way as patients who do not experience it. This is obvious; if one does not have the energy to do everyday things, how could one enjoy occasional activities such as going for a walk, meeting friends or family, going to the movies? And even when you build up the courage to do these things, the fatigue generated by the effort made prevents you from enjoying them. Fatigue does not relate to the severity of the disease.

Fatigue is not the same as drowsiness. People can resolve drowsiness by sleeping, while fatigue may or may not resolve itself by resting, regardless of whether you are sleeping to rest or relaxing, sitting, or lying in an armchair. Some aspects of fatigue may be treatable, either by sleeping more or changing medications, treating depression or through an exercise program.

I still work practically full time, although I quit all my teaching jobs. But I end my work schedule exhausted. When I return home, I often lie down and stay in a mode of disconnection for a while. I do not say asleep because it is not that. Curiously, when I am in that state, I always lie on my back, which is not the position I sleep in. And most of the times I feel better after fifteen minutes. As my neurologist explained to me, in that rest the nervous system restores.

But the thing is that I feel desperate when the need to lie down comes because I can't go on, not even for one more minute. I need to lie down horizontally. I have thrown myself on the floor of a friend's bathroom, sat on the floor during a work meeting (at least I leaned my head against the wall), or I have disappeared from the birthday celebration of one of my daughters hoping my absence will be unnoticed. Later, I gained the strength to ask for a bed to lie down when I am visiting relatives. Also, when there are trust and shared codes, as we agreed with my brother during a trip we did together, a raised hand meant not to expect a response from me right away.

I often describe fatigue as «low bat». This expression is consistent with the one my co-workers use: «Cerruti turned off». The effort required to do daily tasks is so enormous that many times I end up not finding the energy to do them. I agree with the article that fatigue decreases with better rest and physical activity, but does not get along with anxiety, with that state of non-stop, as my husband says.

To a greater or lesser extent, I have symptoms in almost all the categories I listed. Some annoy me but I cope with them, others tire me, others bore me, others mortify me, others embarrass me.

Paradoxically, the ones that affect me the most in my daily life are not the motor symptoms, since I can face them with ingenuity or with help. But no one can help me with difficulty concentrating, with fatigue of the nervous system, or with difficulty expressing myself when I'm tired.

The worst nightmares

Bathing... a grueling experience

Washing my hair leaves me so exhausted that sometimes I need to lie down for a few minutes after bathing. It is one of those repetitive movements that become so difficult, just like brushing, beating, waving with the hand… Trying to overcome the resistance and stiffness of the right arm leaves me more exhausted than an hour of aerobic exercise.

I find the movement of pulling the towel back to dry my back as difficult as a circus stunt.

I help myself with physics; in the summer I let my hair down and my body dry at room temperature. Then I leave my hair wrapped in a towel to absorb the water.

To eat... what a drag

It takes so much effort that laziness takes over... a term I had eradicated from my vocabulary, since -due to the effects of shock and anxiety -, it seemed I didn't need it.

There should be no better recipe for weight loss. I find it difficult cutting food, taking it into my mouth, chewing and swallowing it. When I am hungry, I get desperate struggling with my first bite while others have already finished.

Seconds? I already forgot what that is ... I don't like others to be affected by my slowness. My first dish usually takes up enough time from the others.

One begins to choose what to eat according to the ease or difficulty of cutting it, bringing it to the mouth, or chewing it. Example: I take soup only if I can do it in a cup, rice only when I am at home and I can do it with a spoon, meat only if there is someone who can cut it for me. I think I will always remember the day my youngest daughter offered to cut my food. And I know that swallowing problems have not yet been present.

Oral hygiene... no spectators, please

When I do it in a public bathroom... if I use the electric toothbrush, there is always a person who makes a comment, if I go with the ordinary one I am also not free from comments or looks.

It is clear that: «I brush my teeth and go out» is not a matter of a couple of minutes.

Getting dressed... I love dresses!

It depends on the total challenges I have to confront and how many Parkinson's Friendly choices I have made. It is not that I stop using anything, only that there are days or situations in which I do not have the time, and if I hurry or get stressed, the difficulties increase. I separated a set of accessories for which I do not need help and some outfits... the dresses won by far. In particular, the ones with neither buttons nor zippers, which are wonderful! They have another virtue. Parkinson's disease also affects the ability to make decisions. If I have to start analyzing which blouse for each pair of pants, which belt suits best, etc., I can lose valuable minutes. The dress is a unique garment: nothing to resolve except for some accessories.

Panic attacks

Just imagining some situations scares me. Two in particular: that my handbag could fall and spill out in the middle of the street, and I have to put everything inside in a hurry; and that frozen episode appears at the worst time.

Revolving doors and electric stairs also trigger panic.

Life adjustments

As the disease progresses, there is also the need to incorporate some life adjustments as one accepts the coexistence with «the Englishman».

Winter holidays

My natural medicine doctor strongly recommended it. And I understood immediately. With the chilly weather, rigidity becomes more acute. He also explained to me that in winter there is less energy in the environment.

My family comprehended that, too. The first change occurred soon after the diagnosis and was one thing I reported that Parkinson's gave me: my husband processed his passport for the first time. After the diagnosis I traveled so much with him and my family that I am even a little embarrassed to talk about it. My running shoes have tested international and intercontinental soils.

Personal care

I incorporated the electric toothbrush and adopted a new style with increasingly shorter hair. Also, I had a treatment that allows me to be groomed without using the brush and the hair dryer. The latter requires maneuvers impossible for me.

Clothes and shoes

Although I do not stop using what I like, as I already explained, I have become addicted to dresses.

With shoes, it is another matter. I feel insecure with high heels and I am terrified of falling and hurting myself. And what's worse, fracturing a bone. Among the multiple tests they did for leg pain, I discovered that I have osteoporosis. The very idea of fracturing a bone and not being able to exercise causes me tremendous anguish. I don't want to take the risk. For safety reasons I put aside dressing up and my desire to look a little taller, since I am extremely short.

The other thing that I realize is that it would be easier if I reduce the amount of clothing in the closet, to facilitate its handling. Choosing would be as well simplified. Someday I will do it.

The car

I traded my car for an automatic transmission one. It happened to me that other drivers honked at traffic lights because it took me more time to accelerate. I find it more comfortable and I demand less from my legs. I avoid rush hours and routes where bottlenecks occur. Before I start, I check an application for any accidents or incidents along the way, so I can choose the least stressful route. The combination of the iPhone with the multimedia screen of the car allows me to give directions to the phone without taking my eyes off the road, although I try not to.

Social life

I remember perfectly when a doctor recommended me: «Don't isolate yourself».

And now I think how easy it is to fall into the temptation to isolate myself and stay in the shelter of my home. For starters, in the late afternoon I am often very tired, and going out again does not seduce me in the least. Everything that takes place at this time of day has a prime chance of being canceled.

Also, since getting ready takes a toll on me, I feel lazy. The same with eating, especially the delicious roasts that we eat in my country.

But above all things, it is difficult to overcome depression, apathy, and the desire of wanting nobody to see you.

Work flow

I left it for last. It has been the most difficult and painful adjustment I've made.

On the one hand, I have to admit that for a long time I had longed to work less and that this situation gave me the perfect excuse. It was impossible to follow the care instructions and reduce stress with the large working schedule that I led, which guaranteed neither the night nor the weekend rest. But I also realized that even though I only keep one job, the disease imposed adjustments on the work rhythm.

My neurologist says that the disease does not affect thinking, but slows it down. What I really feel is something else. My head is bursting with all kinds of ideas, but when I am tired

— I should say when I feel that my nervous system is tired or fatigued — I cannot put together the sentences and convey what is clear to me. It is when I have to rest, ideally lie down for ten to fifteen minutes, while I give the nervous system time to recover. It's hard to explain, so I just say: «I'm tired».

I needed to make adjustments for managing other symptoms besides fatigue. I find it very hard to focus and it tires me. To coordinate a meeting can exhaust me if I am repeatedly interrupted. Sometimes I also have a tough time making decisions. But I found that the latter, and the difficulty of expressing myself, improve a lot if I exercise in the morning. So I reserved the first two hours of the day for my care and rehabilitation activities. I organize the agenda so I can breathe between one meeting and the next one. An energy walk between the two perks me up. I exercise, meditate and sleep at least six hours on high exposure days.

Situations that require prior preparation

The queue at the checkout in the supermarket, the line to serve food with a clamp in a hotel, the windows to present documents. To prevent having a bad time, one must assess the situation and plan ahead.

Objects that become dangerous or useless

I cannot move my hands quickly. It makes matches and the steam iron potential sources of accidents. I use a long-handled lighter and an iron without steam.

But I also realize that there are objects that have become useless, like the alarm clock. As my younger brother once said during a trip: «Why do we need an alarm clock to wake up if Florencia is here?».

Help!

Hand in hand with the symptoms are the necessary care practices to mitigate them. It is not about activities to do for a week; one has to integrate them into daily life and perhaps until the last day.

One day I started reciting that list and I got exhausted before I finished it:

«Take the medication at the indicated times four times a day, do aerobic exercise six times a week, build muscle, strengthen the middle area at least five days a week, put eye drops several times a day, do therapy, do foot exercises, do tai-chi, practice yoga, stretch several times a day, meditate, do facial mime exercises, sing, do phonics exercises, take care of the consumption of liquids, take a nap, practice balance postures, get yourself massages and shiatsu, do eye convergence exercises, dance tango, meet people with the same condition…». And the list does not end there. When I finished doing this exercise, I said to myself: «Help!».

On the other hand, just as I know how to see my strengths, I have to admit that my dislike for routines works against me. I am the best at planning and organizing the routines… of others. And mine too, with the detail that when I finish designing them I am already thinking about how to change them or brilliant excuses for not complying with the plan.

And anxiety is a perfect accomplice... What do I mean? To the constant dialogue that the voice of conscience and the voice of anxiety have in my head. Rather than a dialogue, they argue heatedly, with bad words that I cannot repeat here. But basically, these dialogues are something like this:

— You fool, what are you doing on the computer? Don't you know that the only thing that can slow down the progress of the disease is exercising? Let go of that keyboard and go to the club right now!

— I'm coming, it's just that I have five more minutes left.

— What are you doing now? The day is wonderful! Go for a beach run!

— It's that I want to finish sewing this that I want to give to the masseuse.

— Didn't you say that today you would do sit-ups? Are you not aware that you have to strengthen the middle area?

— Yes, yes, but now I am taking advantage of painting these boards, today it is ideal because there is little humidity, I can exercise later.

— Weren't you committed to going to the club every Saturday to build strength?

— It's true, but the grass needs a little raking, I'm still doing some exercise.

Please stop arguing! Can someone turn off the microphone to the voice of anxiety!

Poisons and antidotes

It wasn't long before I knew what the poisons were: stress, intense emotions, cold, lack of sleep or aerobic exercise.

Over time, I was also discovering antidotes. It would be unfair if I didn't top the ranking for antidotes with medication. Today it represents the delay in the need of using a wheelchair in a few years, among many other limitations. But being a neurodegenerative disease, it is necessary to adjust doses and drugs periodically. This is a little scary, but my neurologist from day one reassured me we are just appealing to light artillery, to make sure we still have scope to increase the dose and resort to other options.

The effect is immediately noticeable. With the first pramipexole pills, I could write again. I have a deep respect for this medication. Because it acts on the central nervous system, because of its side effects, because missing the dose can have unpleasant consequences, because quitting these pills for a few days can be dangerous. I also confirm that it is essential to respect the hours when taking them, and the contraindications of combinations with other drugs and the care regarding the time of taking them according to mealtime.

Twice I had incompatibility issues and detected it from how bad I felt! It happened to me with an antibiotic and homeopathy...

Sometimes I'm curious to know what my condition would be without those pills, but I have no intention of checking it.

But this is very dynamic. For now, I am left with the attractive image of my neurologist that there is large artillery we can count on, depending on how the disease evolves. It will have to be adapted to the evolution of the disease. Will a day come when all that artillery not be enough to win the battle? It might be, but I gain nothing from worrying about it now.

Without a doubt, physical exercise occupies number two in the ranking. In the first place, because it is the only thing one can do to slow down the evolution of the disease. But regardless of that medium-term effect, you feel better right away. Exercise is basic in managing depression and anxiety, in improving mental agility, balance, and flexibility, and in decreasing falls.

I confirm that several types of exercises do me good. Those of balance, those of bodybuilding, yoga postures, those of elongation, those of facial mimicry, those of coordination. Also, those of tai-chi, which doctors recommend, since researchers have found that people with Parkinson's who practice it experience fewer falls and have a longer stride length. But I need aerobic exercise as my daily bread. No other exercise can substitute it. My day is completely different when I start it with a brisk walk, running, or dancing.

I must combine medication and physical exercise with something essential such as tools for emotional-psychological balance. I had to hit rock bottom to seek therapy. I remember the day. We had had a day's work at the Estevez Palace and when I left I burst into tears as I said to my co-workers: «I can't take it anymore». And I could have faced nothing if I hadn't taken that step. I also have a prescription from a natural medicine doctor who gave me a lengthy list of recommendations, headed by the prescription for «Silence». It was the strangest prescription I received. How right he was!

When I get up at dawn and scurry to my creativity corner, there are days when I put on music, but there are others when I let my thoughts come out of my head and float in that silence. I observe how they meet, disagree, negotiate, make agreements, and return to their origins only after they have evolved. And later I have to fly to the keyboard, with an urgency equivalent to the urgency to go to the bathroom!

On the psycho-emotional level, various meditation and yoga techniques also helped me. Those minutes, when I accomplish it, are a real investment. The greatest difficulty is overcoming Mrs. Anxiety. But I found out that anxiety drags on longer than I do, and that is not very keen to hammer my head when it just wakes up. I say to myself: «Shhhh, that anxiety has not yet awakened», and I take this opportunity to meditate before it begins with its impertinent questions and prompts.

Some other resources do me a lot of good, such as acupuncture and electroacupuncture, reflexology, bioenergetic massages, and reiki.

On one occasion my boss asked me to accompany him to a television program which made me insecure. I got up at half-past five in the morning and did everything I know works for me to decrease symptoms, both motor and cognitive. I tried not to go to bed as late as I usually do; I did meditation when I woke up; I practiced stretching and aerobic exercises with music to dance to. On the way, I was singing loudly in the car to improve dysphonia and doing facial mime exercises to release the rigidity of the face. A mad woman on the loose, anyone watching might think. At the end of the interview, several friends called me and the collective comment was: «You could notice nothing».

When symptoms no longer go unnoticed

For almost four years I could choose not to say what was happening to me. But there came a time when people started noticing it. They said to me: «You are stiff», «do you have a back problem?», or they made comments about how I brushed my teeth, or how I handled the computer mouse with my left hand. «Swipe the card faster», the supermarket cashier once asked me, a little irritated. I couldn't do it. She ended up passing it for me.

In July we did one of those winter trips, escaping the cold, with my mother and sister. At the beginning of the trip, on the first stop, a security guard told me as he saw me walk: «Mention that you need assistance, don't take the long cue and use the elevator». The situation paralyzed me. About to ask him why he was telling me so, my mother and sister caught up with me. The guard insisted: «Are you together? You should ask for assistance». It was the first time that I had faced such a situation.

Then, going through the scanner, another slightly annoyed guard told me: «Stretch your arms». Obviously, I was not in a good moment; I had slept badly; I felt stressed by everything that the travel preparations had involved: I was taking much longer than I imagined and I was afraid of not finishing on time, and, to top it off... I was excited! Just like kryptonite for Superman... all symptoms accentuated.

My mother started asking for exceptions for me, saying that I was not feeling well. That they let me through earlier, that I shouldn't stand in line. I was crying out loud. Once on the plane, I was begging her not to ask for exceptions on my behalf for what was not strictly necessary. I was also trying to explain her that I was just trying to reach a personal goal of being able to speak naturally about the subject, and that getting to the point of accepting being treated as a person with a disability was a milestone for later. «I am not ready for that exceptional treatment», I said. To which she replied: «And I am not prepared to see you suffer». Faced with that argument, I could not continue. What can you say to a mother who tells you that? It took me six months to answer back. We had a small but healing conversation and then I wrote her a letter which is at the end of these pages.

I think the problem is that no one is prepared to accept disability. As the Argentinian psycho-pedagogue Constanza Orbaiz says, disability does not send you a WhatsApp message saying: «Be prepared, I will arrive in five». It just comes.

No one is prepared. I wasn't. People who love you are not, either. But I recognize that I had not dimensioned how challenging this angle of the encounter with Parkinson's disease could be: accepting that people see me and treat me as a person with a disability.

I experienced a tremendous rejection when a friend asked me why I was not doing the paperwork to obtain a permit to park the car in the handicap spot. It felt like the closest thing to carrying a sign saying: «I am disabled». Surely soon I will think I am a fool not to take advantage of the few benefits people with disabilities have the right to ask for, but for the time being, I can't. However, in my case, I learned afterward a little more, and apparently, I could not even get these benefits. The law considers that it applies to those who suffer from «some important and definitive or transitory deficiency that may last for approximately five years, in the functionality of their limbs». Those living with Parkinson's disease can tell if their limb function is impaired, but they are not among the beneficiaries of this right.

People have no idea of the symptoms associated with Parkinson's disease. I insist that the common people's image is that of an elderly person who trembles. Not much more than that. Sometimes I would love to shout out loud: «I have Parkinson's and that's why all these things happen to me!». It would be so much easier!

How to handle that situation? How to return to the subject of the sharing of the news, four years after the diagnosis? It would take me a long time to answer these questions.

Reaching the eye of the hurricane

I closely followed the news of Hurricane Irma. The images of that entity rotating on an axis at 200 miles per hour captivated me. But I was even more shocked to know that calm reigned inside the eye.

That's how I felt when I burst with anxiety: swept away by winds of 200 miles per hour, unable to stop turning and turning. There was no way to cross the arms of the hurricane to slow it down and disarm it in the peace of its eye.

I have no doubt that exercise is a powerful anxiolytic and that it works wonders for me. But the winds propelled me in other directions. Or I would start exercising and finish earlier to start another task. I was aware that sleeping was vital. I intended to go to bed early, but the winds prevented me from doing so.

I had to figure out the way to disarm the hurricane, or at least to get to his eye. To my mind comes the time I was working in the Presidency of the Republic. On days of great storms, wind gusts would hit Plaza Independencia so hard that on several occasions they placed a rope to cross the street. Besides, there were police or firefighters who accompanied the risky pedestrians during the crossing holding the rope. That's what I needed: a rope to cross the winds and several strong friendly arms to lean on.

The first step I took was to listen once more to my body, recognizing that I had crossed the codes of coexistence and admitted to having trespassed the threshold of what is tolerable. My instinct led me to search through my medication, and I was not mistaken.

Once I corrected the medication incompatibility, I went out of overflow anxiety mode and made an appointment with my psychiatrist. She listened to me at length despite the few minutes that the health system allocates to each appointment. Together we evaluated changes in medication. The first one sounded ideal, but I felt lousy. The second plan is working and I notice a slow but positive progressive trend.

Another significant change was to identify the cause of leg pain and eliminate it. After several months, I found a physical therapist that by just watching my walk, could tell me I needed to correct the position of my foot or I would have knee pain and then hip pain. To which I replied: «I already have hip pain!». Obviously, without realizing it, the stiffness in my right leg was causing me to turn my foot inward. Creepy basics. All my gait and my musculoskeletal system affected by a few degrees off center. It caused a pain that disabled me for months and that conditioned my coexistence with the disease and therefore my quality of life. For two weeks I left work at midday to do physiotherapy sessions with ultrasound applications and to learn to stretch and do exercises to walk correctly. In a brief time, the pain disappeared. I can never stop thanking Claudia for the turn she gave to the panorama I was in.

Another angel on my way was the body therapist with mastery of the techniques of reflexology, shiatsu, reiki, and bioenergetic massage. On one occasion I got off the stretcher and said: «I have no pain!». I came to my house and was parading to show my husband how well I was walking. Another time, while massaging a few points on my back, I watched in amazement as my right arm moved by itself and stretched out on the table. One day, after she applied shiatsu maneuvers to my right leg, I said: «Ileana, I feel like my leg is longer». «Yes», she replied, «three centimeters longer». No medication had achieved such results.

Although the effects were not permanent, I gradually improved. Besides, it was the only moment when I disconnected and rest deeply; my breathing became imperceptible as I gave myself to those expert hands that converse with my body. And that was a balm to offset the effects of my state of anxiety, which led me to never stop... When she finishes I don't want to leave, and I often ask her, jokingly, if she doesn't offer a full board.

What always works for me when I get to do it, is meditation. Concentrating on breathing as I let thoughts pass by, just watching them. The effect is evident.

I also noticed that I sleep better after starting to apply a few drops of lavender oil under my nose.

They were a set of different significant signs of progress, but they barely allowed me to take refuge from the strongest winds. Anxiety has slightly diminished, but apathy and extreme fatigue were busy doing their homework.

Later I realized that I was going to war with a fork and I understood why a specialist I consulted told me: «You shouldn't be petty with levodopa, when the patient needs it, doctors must prescribe it».

Running out of fuel

Everything is uphill for me. It is as if every muscle I intend to move has to overcome a stiff resistance. As if I had to unclench my vocal cords to pronounce each word. As if there is a lack of grease in the gears I need to set in motion to express my thoughts. It tires me. It bummes me. It irritates me. It bores me. It exhausts me. It makes me don't want to do what is not essential.

I try to exercise and the image in the mirror is so awkward that I don't recognize myself. It discourages me from continuing to try.

I feel like I crawl to work. I return to my house in rubles. Sometimes I arrive hungrily, but my energy is not enough to do everything. To avoid preparing a tea I choose to eat just something solid. Everything I do requires a cold decision. Will I brush my teeth before going to bed? What if I don't put on my pajamas and fall asleep dressed as I am? Sometimes I avoid intervening in a conversation if it is not absolutely necessary, because of the effort that speaking means when I am exhausted.

One day I told my husband I was thinking of quitting work. Once again he told me that he supported my will if that was what I wanted. But I knew there was a good chance I would regret it later.

At the next appointment with the neurologist, I mentioned how I felt. The significant effort that implied for me to do everything. How mortified I feel at needing help to cut my food. He asked some questions about what consequences those symptoms had in my daily life. He took the prescription book while explaining that we would continue with the same medication for now. But as I was leaving, I said to him: «Doctor; I don't think I can continue working. I'm exhausted». And just then I heard him say: «In that case, we will prepare to move forward to another stage of treatment.»

At the next appointment with my neurologist, I was alone. He asked me to make the precise hand movements he monitors at each appointment. I, almost tearfully, said: «I can't». He reassured me by saying: «Don't think the disease is worsening, think of it as you're running out of fuel». That day was the end of the pre-levodopa era. And the fuel that I was running out of finally arrived.

PART IV

The others

A former co-worker asked me to write this chapter. She is a Psychologist and has a degree in Communication. I never told her, but she was the first person to ask me what was wrong with my back and to which I bluntly answered: «I have Parkinson's, didn't you know?». Well, she didn't know and as a first experience, it wasn't very good. She was paralyzed, and it took her several days to write to me in return about the subject. But because of this episode, I shared my writing progress with her and she is becoming a dedicated «editorial consultant». She has told me that what I write looks like a manual for medical psychology and that there is nothing more pedagogical than this book. She encouraged me to keep writing as she believes it can help others a lot and asked me to write a chapter for those that do not have Parkinson's but somehow are close to someone who does. She told me it was uncommon to find these kinds of ideas coming from someone with the disease. In gratitude, I dedicate not a chapter, but an entire part of the book, hoping to meet her expectations.

Who are the others?

Under the term «the others» I will refer not only to those who accompany, but rather to the whole family, friends, co-workers, or those who share a journey, people in general. Included in «the others» are that strange set of health professionals that follow my progress in the disease.

I will start by saying that, from where I stand, there are several common denominators in «the others», which have to do with what I have reflected on:

- Little or nothing is known about the disease. The large group restrict the disease to the elderly and only associate tremor as a symptom. Even many health professionals I have dealt with are reluctant to accept the diagnosis. It is difficult then to pretend that ordinary people can recognize your particular symptoms as Parkinson's.

- I think there is great illiteracy in the language of emotions; we freeze, we don't know what to say, we panic at the other's response, at saying something out of place or making a mistake. As a born researcher, I sometimes think I might have a lot of fun doing some experiments on how people react when I break the news. But my black humor doesn't go that far.

- The sad observation of the relevance of time. Today we measure almost everything based on the time it takes.

And patience is a virtue that few cultivate. People always seem to be in a hurry, they don't want to wait; they get impatient in the lines, at the traffic lights, in the airports, in the restaurants, and the rush does not go well with Parkinson's.

An army in search
of its commander in chief

I tried to find a suitable name for the group of health professionals who care for me. But all the ones I found involved teamwork, the recognition of a leader... but I don't feel that any of these describes the group of specialists who follow me.

My fingers are not enough to count them: neurologist, psychiatrist, physiatrist, sports medicine, psychologist, physiotherapist, endocrinologist, acupuncturist, natural medicine doctor, homeopath, body therapist, rheumatologist, eye doctor, dermatologist...

Of course — like any woman — I also have to go to the gynecologist and the general doctor! When? At the health service, they insist that I go to the check-up with my head doctor. I know that I have to do it. I reply that I will go, but that at this moment I am going to the facility every week; have mercy!

It would be so wonderful if this diverse group of expert people functioned as a true team!

But I'm not complaining. I have to admit that I receive very special treatment even though I don't have any private insurance. Doctors dedicate more minutes than the assigned per patient. Everyone remembers my case and most of them call me by name. Many have given me their mobile phone numbers. They have told me to go to them if I need to take a leave-of-absence, that they can see me in their off-duty hours, that they can give me access notes to an appointment if there is no one available, that they will write notes to the Directorate so I can receive the medications that I need and that the institution is not obliged to provide to me.

I am also aware of the relevance of the vision and the contributions of non-medical professionals. In the first place, I don't know where I would be if I hadn't faced therapy with a psychologist. None of the several doctors who saw me could detect what the physiotherapist saw on the first appointment and that stopped the pain that had been bothering for several months. None of the medications prescribed by the neurologist gives me the effect that the body therapist sometimes achieves.

I know that the response I have from the professionals who care for me is due, in part, to my attitude. On one occasion the psychiatrist told me that just by seeing me in the waiting room she could tell that I was better. To which I told her I had gotten up at six in the morning to do a little exercise at home, actually to dance, because that helped me the entire day and was what she had noticed. She replied: «You are outstanding!». And she went on to tell me about an experience she had earlier with a patient that all she expected from her was a medical certification. On another occasion, the acupuncturist told me she loved receiving me because I always had good news.

But I also feel that there is certain compassion in the attitude of these professionals. Perhaps because many are close to my age and can identify with my situation. Perhaps because, no matter how much they work in the health sector, they do not stop wondering what they would do if they were diagnosed with a neurodegenerative disease.

I feel like they connect emotionally with me. The acupuncturist got goosebumps when I told her I was writing and it happened again when I told her I had finished as a finalist in a short story literary contest on Parkinson's. The body therapist's eyes filled with tears as she told me she had come across her name in a preliminary version of my book I shared with her. The expression on the neurologist's face lit up when I told him about my book.

It is clear that in this process my GP is my neurologist. I consult with him about almost everything and I have blind confidence in him. He was so careful with the diagnosis that with my husband we had to go over what he had said. I recorded in my memory several of the messages he gave me that day, although it took me time to decode them. And as I did it, I realized how perfect his choice was. He stressed the importance of getting to know the disease, of doing physical activity at a competitive training level, that I should take psychological therapy at the beginning, but that it would not be necessary forever. He looked at my husband and told him not to do things for me and to avoid tension at home. He reassured me about the wide range of medication alternatives and how much research is progressing in this field and from which I will surely benefit in the near future. The only thing I remember saying was: «I will not die from this, am I?». At least I said something. My husband was speechless.

Anyway, and from a distance, I find it crazy to send people home with such a diagnosis, trying to figure out what they were told, trying to figure out what they were told, where and how to proceed, what steps to take, in what order, with whom, how to communicate the news. Besides, I realize that there are two different scenarios: the early-onset Parkinson's disease that finds you in the prime of life, with children in your care, at the peak of your career, and the Parkinson's diagnosed after this stage.

Many times I thought it would have been very useful for me to have at least been given a booklet with the ABC´s, if only for the period immediately after diagnosis. Keep in mind that one is in a state of shock and that it is in this state that one will have to make decisions, communicate the news and start acting. It surprised me when four years after the diagnosis I found a booklet from Canada in which patients with early-onset Parkinson's provided recommendations for others. I couldn't feel more identified with the advice expressed there! All my knowledge from this time was reflected there! How much effort could I have saved if I had found this information earlier!

I realize that I guide my treatment. I propose, I discuss, I evaluate, I suggest. If I hadn't mentioned it to my neurologist, he wouldn't have given me the pass for the acupuncturist appointment. If I hadn't asked my body therapist for shiatsu maneuvers, she might never have applied them to me. If I hadn't told the acupuncturist I knew about the evidence for electroacupuncture and had already tried it, perhaps at that time, she would have just applied dry acupuncture.

So, there is a leader from that set of professionals, ¡that leader is oneself! That army has its commander-in-chief.

I don't want to end this chapter without paying special recognition to my neurologist. I want to thank him infinitely for a small giant gesture he had with my mother. She consulted with him on a personal matter and mentioned that I was her daughter. He replied that of course he recalled me and said: «Your daughter is a winner». Five words. Three seconds, maybe. Only expected of a great human being who understood what that mother needed to hear and had the generosity to tell her so.

Ideas to accompany
that should not fail

Everyone wants to help, but nobody knows how. The news has also affected them. And they become desperate for doing something. You don't even know what you need and much less can put it into words. There are no recipes, but in the course of these past four years, I have wondered what were those attitudes or gestures that I appreciated or that would have been good for me, and that I have a feeling that should work most times.

I suppose that, as the disease progresses, I will identify other things, but I also suppose that many of these ideas thought for the first post-diagnosis years can also work for later stages. I describe them from my experience as a woman. We have talked a lot with my husband about this topic, and I realize he does not share some of these ideas. Perhaps men, by nature or by social construction, operate differently, particularly in the face of what makes them vulnerable. Surely also, what each person needs is different. Having made these assessments, I share what in my case helped me, or I think it would have helped me. I believe these ideas can help both those who accompany and those who suffer from the disease to understand their needs. I relate it to those who accompany a friend, but this friend may be the partner or other family member. I also will relate your friend as a «he» just to simplify the reading, but he could be a «she».

Unconditional love, pampering, and encouragement

- Knowing you are unconditionally loved gives a lot of strength. Don't miss your chance to let him know. But since your friend will not always want to talk, a good idea is to send a brief message to his phone: «Thinking of you, I am sending you a hug». Frequently, but not overwhelmingly. You can't imagine how welcome it will be, although you probably won't have an answer.

- Think that self-esteem falters. Be sure to praise something he did well, how fantastic he looks, or to recognize an effort. On one occasion a friend told me she did not point out these things to me because she thought I didn't need it. It must be what I convey, but it is just enough to place yourself in your friends' shoes for a minute to realize that self-esteem is seriously threatened.

- If you are the partner, let him know you find him or her attractive. It is a way of saying that you still see the person who is suffering from these symptoms, but not the symptoms.

- Show him he is special to you. Give him a little gift. It implies that you have him in your thoughts.

Are you really willing to listen? Be explicit with words and deeds.

- If you want to know how your friend is, don't ask him: «How are you?». Use another expression that clarifies that you are willing to listen. It can be: «how are you doing with your things?», or directly: «have you been to the doctor lately?», «How are you doing?». Never do it in front of third parties, unless you are sure it is not a problem. A few days ago, the housekeeper who has worked at home for many years, while we were alone at the house and I was calmed, asked me: «How are you?», and after a slight pause, she continued... «regarding your condition?». I am amazed at her wisdom.

- Don't expect him to open up in a sizeable group. Offer him instances to chat in pairs. Especially at first, keep in mind that he will probably want to cry, and not all places are suitable for doing so. He might not want to speak for fear of not being able to hold back tears.

- Don't expect that if you call him on the phone he will tell you what's wrong. He might not always want his children or partner to listen.

Get informed to accompany, to offer resources, to understand their decisions

- Find out about his condition. Don't make him explain everything. The National Parkinson's Foundation, the American Parkinson's Disease Association, The Michael J. Fox Foundation, and the Muhammad Ali Parkinson Center are excellent resources for people with Parkinson's disease, their families, and those they accompany.

- Offer him the resources that you think can help him and pave the way. On one occasion I asked a friend whom she bought organic products. I was interested in this topic since I know about the neurotoxic effect of pesticides and their association with the disease. She suggested I call a mutual friend who was the one who passed the contact to the provider. I never called her. I was having a troublesome time thinking about the conversation that I knew would take place. I just needed the provider's phone number!

- Do not push or get angry if he doesn't follow your advice. Perhaps it is not the right moment; perhaps he cannot cope with everything, but be certain that somewhere he will thank you. It is possible that when your friend has the strength or he feels that the time is right, he will take up your suggestions.

- Remember that intense emotions are to the person with Parkinson's what kryptonite is to Superman... They weaken them, they hurt them; they exacerbate their symptoms... It is possible that if he had reached a precarious balance, these powerful emotions, but also the stress unbalanced him. So don't insist if he doesn't want to attend a heartbreaking funeral or a trial hearing, or get involved in a difficult or painful argument. It does him a lot of harm.

Show him a way to get the shame out of the way

- Help him speak about it naturally. You can take the first step towards taking away the shame or secret connotation of the disease. When you are alone with him, name the disease. Instead of asking: «Does the disease have to do with your dysphonia?», ask: «Does Parkinson's have to do with your dysphonia?» Later, perhaps you can also do it in front of others if your friend agrees.

- Laugh *with* your friend about ridiculous situations, but never, never make fun *of anyone* who has some kind of disability. That hurts a lot. For example, your friend comes walking with something in his hands that falls and everything rolls on the floor without control. If your friend laughs at the situation, you can laugh with him. If he feels like crying, it is out of the question.

- Another thing that does well is to bring into dialogue the lives of people who successfully deal with the disease or with any disability. Who everybody admires for what they are, and that when you look at them, you see past the disability. For example, Pope John Paul II. I reflected on this when I saw the coach of the Uruguayan soccer team with his canes. The man is the best at what he does. Who can see disability in him?

These examples can show your friend that the disease does not define us, that you can move on, that there is nothing to be ashamed of.

Did you find out your friend's diagnosis and you do not know how to approach him?

Again, the answer will depend on your friend. Once again, my husband and I don't agree. He would prefer that no one talk about Parkinson's. But this issue has a lot to do with the connotation of a secret or shameful situation.

I think the best thing is to let your friend know that you are aware of the news. Returning to the housekeeper, when she found out about my diagnosis, she sent me a text message that moved me and that I have saved. She told me bluntly how sad she was and how much she valued me. And I kept thinking she was the only person who used that resource that I appreciated so much. Nobody — and when I say nobody is nobody — sent me a message of the type: «Flor, I was told what you're going through, you can count on me for anything, be strong!». They only talked to me about my diagnosis after I had told them myself. I wonder why. I think the answer is for delicacy, for respect, for not intruding, for not knowing if I wanted to speak about it or if I wanted to keep it in reserve. But the fact is that you have found out, and your friend should know that you are aware. You avoid him trying to guess if you know or not, or if he has to find the moment to tell you.

Finding a suitable time to tell others the news was one of the more difficult things I had to cope with. Mainly because I learnt from first experiences that I couldn't predict their reactions. As I said before, I came across with others´ tears, denials, skipping to another topic...and with my own tears too! And many times, after I had planned the moment and taken courage, I would tell someone the news, and they would say: «I knew it...». So I ask you to be condescending to your friend and let him know that you are aware.

By this way your friend would not need to hide his symptoms to prevent an awkward moment of questioning. This situation sometimes led me, for example, to refuse a cup of coffee even if I wanted to have it. It also reduces the amount of talk of what happens to you, something I often found myself trying to guess what was like. And with the idea of not reminding him of his condition... one appreciates the intention, but Parkinson's accompanies you from the moment you get up in the morning until you get up the next day, nights included, such as the 24-hour reminder survey technique. There is no chance that your friend will forget.

I think there's some confusion: it is one thing to respect that your friend does not want to detail the symptoms he has or to relate the emotions that this diagnosis has caused him, and another thing is to make the subject taboo. You can talk about it naturally, accepting that the disease is part of your friend's day to day, from now on his path companion, without having to dig into the pain that it produces if he doesn't feel like doing it.

Do not overprotect, do not press, be inclusive, and... arm yourself with patience!

- Let him take care of himself in everything he can do. He has enough frustration with what he truly cannot do. Do not offer to carry his suitcases if that does not cause him problems; offer to fasten the necklace or open the sugar sachet.

- Arm yourself with patience and show that you have no problem with the time that things take. I bless when a cashier tells me: «Don't worry, I'm here until six o'clock», while I try to save all the documents and tickets.

- Offer help in what you think he may need, without pressing. And always ask first. Will you let me help you cut the food and are you done fighting? Enable yes and no in response. Receiving a «no» for an answer does not mean that on another occasion he will accept your help gladly.

- In group instances, go ahead and distribute the tasks so he can do some. There's no need to expose him to do what he finds difficult or to put him in the situation of having to explain that he cannot. That eases a lot. Don't suggest that he serve the food! For example, you can ask him to bring the bread basket, take photos, or play music.

Put yourself in his shoes to avoid unlucky comments or attitudes

I know that people generally have the best of intentions. But I would like you to see that not all good intentions derive from the intention that motivated them. I will give some examples.

- Don't try to comfort him by trying to minimize what is happening to him. Don't do a drama, either. Listen and try to imagine what he feels. You may be tempted to say something like: « I've been told that there is a lot of medication for Parkinson's now and that it is not like before, there is nothing to worry about». But you need to understand that his life changed with the diagnosis, that he has a neurodegenerative, evolutionary, chronic, and without cure disease, that he doesn't know what the future has for him. The current medication indeed changes perspectives, but if you tell him: «Everything will be fine and there is nothing to worry about», you will stop being a valid confidant and he will surely stop opening up with you.

- Don't affirm: «I understand you» or «I know how you feel» because your friend knows that you've never been through the same thing and that no matter how hard you try, you can't know what he's feeling. You should listen to him and try to understand him. «I'm listening to you», «I'm here for you», «Is there anything I can do for you?» may be better answers.

- Don't feel obligated to give advice. Don't be afraid of silence, you don't always have to say something. Often the best thing you can do for your friend is simply listen to him or accompany him.

- Don't watch him, nobody likes to feel watched. It is different if you do it without him noticing, just to be aware of how the disease is developing.

- If you have old stories, things you didn't like, anger, don't insist if he doesn't want to talk about it. He might be weak. Maybe it makes him feel bad. Maybe the person you are angry at doesn't exist anymore.

- Pity is the last thing one wants to awaken in the other. But pity is not equivalent to care, pampering, or some privileges that one experiences them as blessings. There are minor gestures that bring in incredible time gain and immeasurable energy savings. An offer to hand me a cup of coffee was long interpreted within my team as a pimp act towards the boss. Luckily the «gutter detector», as I call it, now has a higher threshold. I sigh with joy when they realize what I need and they give it to me. I remember very well once, when coordinating a team meeting, I started to feel fatigued. I looked at the couch which I go to under these circumstances, but they had left a lot of things on it. The most intuitive of my team, saying nothing, got up and released the couch so I could follow the meeting from there, more comfortable, with my head back. How can we not bless those gestures?

Help him not isolate himself

- Your friend will have a thousand excuses to avoid social life. A thousand reasons to get depressed. Engage with him in activities you know he likes, at the time and in the way that work best for him.

- Exercise does a lot of good. Share a walk or join his routine in whichever way you can.

- Encourage him to do tasks he likes. Talk to him about these topics.

Will you spend a few days together? Have a few words before you do.

It is easier if you make some specifications and previous agreements. What do you have to know about their routines, their medications, what to do «in case of». What does he need your help for, which is not the same as asking him if he needs your help.

I learned this after a trip with my mother and sister because I didn't do it. It was in the pre-levodopa era.

I should have previously told them:

- I need to do things without being rushed. So I prefer to be the last to get on the plane and the last to get off. That allows me not to get tired waiting in long lines, not to get nervous trying to settle into the seat while other passengers wait impatiently.

- I have no problem loading my bags.

- I need help to cut the food. I thank you for offering it to me and accept my answer.

- I must respect the hours when I have to take my medications. Some I also have to take based on meals.

- Sometimes I cannot describe the magnitude and kind of tiredness I experience. If I say: «I am very tired», I need to stop and rest for fifteen minutes or return to the hotel without delay. Please don't ask me to stop for a photo.

- Don't worry if I fall asleep dressed. Sometimes I don't have the energy to change. But since I wake up several times at night, the next time I wake up I will put on my pajamas and brush my teeth. It's not that bad.

After understanding this, I took a trip with my mother, this time accompanied by my younger brother. Upon arrival at the destination, on the way to the hotel, I said that it would be a good idea if each one explained what they needed from the others because of their health conditions. On this occasion I was already taking levodopa, so my requirements were different. Everything I had to say impressed me, while I realized that it was an opportunity to share many details of my illness that they were interested in knowing.

In this way they became my allies to remind me to take the medications at the necessary times, we planned the time of the meals to respect the time I had to leave after taking the levodopa, they did not insist on loading my suitcases, but rather they asked me to help them with theirs, they did not mind that I returned to the hotel before they did.

Do you have a co-worker who has Parkinson's?

Think about the workplace as a privileged environment to treat the disease naturally. You will meet every day, you will be able to notice how the symptoms develop and you will also live with your friend's new route companion. Sometimes this situation is not even achieved in the house itself, where one also takes care to not worry their loved ones.

But I also know that it is difficult for you to imagine the effort your friend makes to keep working. Either because of what it means to go through the stages of shock and acceptance, or because of the disease itself, everything is more difficult now. Also, it may be difficult for him to accept that he cannot handle everything as before.

Surely your friend will want to free himself of some responsibilities that especially tire him, or that he cannot undertake as before and that make him a bottleneck. If the work dynamic allows it, talk to him looking for alternative tasks he could perform so he could feel valued in what he is truly good at, and delegate what others can do.

Your friend may fear the time when he is no longer in a position to continue working. And also fear that others will notice it first. Therefore, include him in the proposals to change his tasks. Otherwise, your friend will question whether the measures are aimed at making things easier for him or if the underlying reason is that you no longer think he can carry them out. Even if this is the case, it is better to address it directly.

Also, ask him how he wants to handle the news of the illness with others, and offer to pave the way if he wants to. That means a lot more help than you think.

As I was saying, it is difficult to imagine the effort he is making. It is good that you consider it. If among the job changes your friend happened to occupy a place of less visibility or public exposure, he might feel hurt to have become invisible. When you have the opportunity, publicly recognize his contributions, even if he made them from the shadows.

Nothing to explain to you: other people with Parkinson's

Shortly after the diagnosis, I made a shy attempt to contact Parkinson's groups in my country. I didn't receive an immediate response and I didn't insist. My neurologist also warned me that perhaps, as a recently diagnosed patient, it could affect me to see other people in advanced stages of the disease, and he stressed that my symptoms did not necessarily go so far.

So five years passed and I had had no contact with anyone who had the disease. My only relationship had been a sparse virtual link through online patient forums, Facebook pages, and two words by chatting with the author of a book.

I have a lot to thank the former co-worker who introduced me to a friend of hers. She told me we shared not only the diagnosis but a multiplicity of personal characteristics. I also recognize her guts; many would have preferred not to take the risk. I hadn't even made time to go meet her newborn daughter, but she never said anything about it.

I realized at the time that I had never spoken to anyone in my condition. Straightaway I said yes. My friend told me that he was active at work and that we had a lot in common. I perfectly remember the first words on Whatsapp. He said to me: «I have been reluctant to group by illness, but I will make an exception for you». Not a week passed that the three of us were already at my friend's house having tea and exchanging experiences and life teachings, boldly. Like two friends who haven't seen each other for five years. And we started a verbose dialogue on WhatsApp, in which I found myself laughing out loud.

We were perplexed and hilarity at the similarity of personalities despite having had so many different life experiences, shared emotions, and identical paths. Perhaps that permitted us to say things to each other with unimaginable harshness, missing nothing, because as similar as we were, it was impossible to deceive each other. The most incredible thing was when he told me that he had read my progress and that, despite everything I said, I was still a perfectionist and not very humble person. And even a little pedantic! He described me saying that I seemed to say: «I arrived, I am here, listen to me, do not waste what I have to tell you». I burst out laughing, unable to stop, for an entire week. Never, but never, had someone ever said something like that to me. For my part, I did not stay behind when I made some sharp interpretations of things that he told me.

Not only did we turn out to be like separated at birth, but to top it off, we fit like two pieces of a puzzle. One day I mentioned to him about my concern to form a group of young actively working people. I was convinced that it would do me good and that there would be others who would also be needing it. I thought about how good it would be to accompany and motivate each other in the daily challenge of living with the disease. He was immediately excited by the idea.

From the club, while running on the treadmill, I dictated the objectives of the group. The general and the specific ones. The participants' profile. The meeting dynamics. He wrote it on his home computer and was in charge of making the calls to the possible interested parties that we would have to find. An explosive pair.

The proposal came together on more than fertile ground. Of each one we invited, the first thing we received was a: «Yes! I want to participate!». And when we got together, just a week after I started dreaming about the idea, I realized why. Each of us was living the disease surrounded by people who loved us but in absolute solitude.

And in this way, like companions of a presidential formula, we founded the group of seven. Or of the eight and we go for more. We were seduced by the objectives of meeting and accompaniment, of sharing and having fun, of collaborating in adherence to treatment. To meet each other, without the mediation of a facilitator.

The effect of the encounter was magical. For multiple reasons. For the surprise of the similarity of profiles. For the emotions aroused. The first time we met the most repeated phrases were: «It happens to me too»; «I have nothing to explain to you». That was such a relief! It was so weird and yet so easy! There was something that caught my attention: despite what I had read so much and convinced myself that there are as many Parkinson's pictures as there are people who suffer from it, our symptoms were surprisingly similar.

I admit that I had not dimensioned the need for this meeting until I experienced it. Personally, I learned and I was filled with support and courage. As I listened to them, sharing how they traveled with issues such as hiding or not their symptoms, asking or not to be helped at an airport, or why to stop teaching if that is what one likes…. I thought how difficult it is to take a stand on these issues alone!

A very particular group: an internist, a pediatrician, a cardiologist, a nutritionist, a lawyer, an economist, and an educator. But more are on the way: a former businessman, a social worker. Virtually all of us were or had been teachers. Particular and select. But it wasn't because we looked for it like that. When we define the participants´ profile, obviously we never thought about a professional title or academic career! Quite simply, they were the names that came up with just a few questions in our immediate circle. I was stunned to know how many people were so close under the same circumstances.

There are the doctors, who say that they are not treated like patients when they need to be, because of their condition, especially by their peers.

Some are going through the mourning of their retirement process, bearing the label of «totally inept» or «incapacitated for any type of task».

There are also those of us who juggle to continue working. And when the overflow of creativity assails me, I start to think about everything that could be done from a hypothetical *Parkinson's worker support unit* for those who resist the temptation to appeal to early retirement. Armchairs for a 30-

minute nap? Assistants, to write in medical records or prescriptions? There could be so many resources!

Between us, there is nothing to explain. However, I feel that there is much to explain outwards. I constantly wonder if anyone has thought about what the person who receives the opinion of «totally inept» or «incapacitated for any type of task» feels. I know what the retirement grounds say, but will there be no other alternative? Has anyone thought that there are people with disabilities who do not want to identify themselves with a wheelchair as a symbol? In the case of Parkinson's disease, it implies having reached the last stage of the disease, which nobody wants to reach. Has anyone thought that young people with Parkinson's may want to continue working, but that everything leads to early retirement?

There is much to do and I intend to do something about it.

Reading, writing
and sharing with others

Reading involves tremendous effort for me, because of the difficulty to concentrate and because anxiety rings in my head asking: «What else can I do now?». However, some readings caught and inspired me. They helped me understand many things. Not everything is under our control and that we walk through life convinced that what defines us are roles that we acquire (The key to the good life, by Joan Garriga). To see clearly that you can and that everything is a matter of attitude (A life without limits, by Nick Vujicic). To reflect on what is truly important in life (Living is an urgent matter and Reinventing yourself, by Mario Alonso Puig). To understand many things around the process of illness and healing (Energy Medicine, by Caroline Myss).

As soon as I began to write I realized that I had discovered the most remarkable therapeutic tool. I had to admit to my troubled perfectionism its fundamental role for it, acting as an implacable judge of the expression of my feelings. It was a four-year process interrupted only at times by overflowing anxiety and mixed emotions.

The richness of the experience was not only writing but what was generated when I began to share what I wrote.

Without realizing when I made the change, I started sharing my drafts with other types of people. People not as close or who were going through situations similar to mine, although not exclusively with a diagnosis of Parkinson's. I also continued the dialogue with some readers of the first chapters. The reviews of this draft version of the project were different from the first ones.

Some who had read the first drafts, when they came across this latest version, sighed with relief: «This time I was not furious with life and its injustices like the previous time! Everything came together with infinite peace! What a privilege to be your friend; what a privilege that you have chosen me as a path companion; what a privilege to be part of your memory!».

Almost without exception, reading got readers emotional, while at the same time it made them smile. «I cried the whole book... and I smiled with hope all the time». «I was surprised many times with a smile on my face». «Still drying my tears from the spectacular letters, I count myself as an admirer in your army!». «I will need not a handkerchief, but a bedsheet to read everything you write. I don't know how your mother will manage it». «I finished reading your book. To think that I began reading it from an editorial point of view, but after the first chapter, I continued reading with my soul and shedding many emotional tears».

Everybody told me they felt trapped by the reading. «I didn't read your book... I devoured it!». I have devoured your book! I will do it many more times». «Flor, I began to read your book and it is difficult for me to stop reading, something that only happens to me when they touch deep inside of me. It is fresh, human, sincere, and spontaneous. You transmit what you want, you get hooked on the story, it is harmonious». «Your way of expressing your experiences caught me! It brings people very close and humanizes the «Englishman», as you say. It makes you live it so vividly! It generates a lot of empathy». «You know I started reading and so far I can't stop».

Many pointed out the honesty poured into these pages: «I will continue to take the time this torrent of honesty and courage deserves». «It's almost a confession!». «The valor of the person who writes — valor in the sense of courage — is that of not making any kind of concession. Pure and simple truth. And that gives it great credibility. The succession of daily events and their associated feelings lead the reader along the path of human drama. Of losses, of limitations, of resignations. Those that we all have, that which touches us or will do?».

They highlighted having their feelings and experiences reflected in words, something they could not do. And to see themselves in the mirror through these pages even when they don't have Parkinson's. «There are clear ideas that I can never put into words... It is like reading my life, but with different circumstances. I am ashamed to say that I am in a deep depression that prevents me from going to work. Why does it embarrass me? Reading your book was like looking at myself in a mirror. «I think this book is not just for people who have Parkinson's, or relatives with Parkinson's. Your words go beyond your illness. I have other health conditions and this book touched my soul». «Many of your experiences are just like mine in another context. Your mourning, the feeling that everything is turned upside down, of seeking diagnoses, of being the leader of a multidisciplinary team that you end up forming, of the others who also suffer, but until we can reactivate ourselves we cannot see it; fear, anxiety and many more things that we can share from afar and in Montevideo when we see each other on my next visit. I read it and I see your change. Wishing to spend an afternoon chatting with you!».

They also referred to intensity. «It is not a study book that can be read critically, skip paragraphs, and read only what is important. I am not a good reader. In your book, if I skip a paragraph, I miss an important part, so I prefer to go slowly and highlight it to read it again the next day». «It is a story of great intensity. At times devastating. At times, highly inspiring.».

They valued the way of conveying the experiences. «It is incredible how you managed to convey your experiences in such a natural, transparent, and graphic way!». «I just wish I could do as you do; you transform feelings, smells, landscapes, colors into words and I want your book to be a total success». «You express all the things that I feel and that have happened to me and I don't know how to do it as you do». «Impressive how you write, you pass on something incredible!».

I am increasingly encouraged to publish it. «I think those who suggest you publish are right. I think it is a book that many people will thank you for!». «It is incredible, in our profession (psychology) one does not stop studying, we even study how to accompany these situations, how to accompany family members, and there is indeed nothing more informative, more illustrative, more pedagogical than this book! It looks like a manual for medical psychology!». «I think it's a very good resource for doctors, for medical students». «You have to publish it! Your way of conveying all of this is very valuable». «It hooked me so much that it makes me want it to be published and start to be read by everyone who is touched in some way by similar topics». « It seems to me basic literature for the health care staff, for the families of people with Parkinson's disease, for friends, even for supermarket cashiers… in short, for people who are so important to the bearer!». «It would also be a very good source, due to its sensitivity, for those who plan a public social campaign about certain conditions». «This is an excellent inclusion manual!». «I am so glad you used this writing skill, I know it is very therapeutic to do so, but do not doubt that it is also very therapeutic to read!». «What a great, enormous, and courageous decision you made to write your experience. That is being brave!».

They also told me what it left or can leave to whoever reads it. «I have learned a lot from this reading about panic attacks. It will help me with my patient, but it is not the most important thing that it has given me». «The meticulous detail of the strategies that the rapporteur deploys, highlights the value of the miracle of life. It teaches that life always finds its way. The family impact, the new rearrangements, the role changes. The intense love that surely returns and protects as it has been loved and protected so many times. The whole story transmits determination, work, effort, self-control». «From adversity, the person achieves unthinkable things for those who are not in that place, and for this reason it causes admiration. Then, it could be thought that your story is a valuable guide for those who suffer from Parkinson's. Because it gathers a very important amount of information and strategies for daily life. But above all, because it is a factual demonstration that it is possible to move on».

And finally, I found some messages like this last one that reached my soul: «Oh, Florcita! The first thing I did was to print what you sent me to read at home, and I couldn't stop reading it at the office! It fills my soul; how successful you are! Successful even in the face of adversity. You move me to the core of my being, and you give me life lessons with every word you write here. You are not teaching anymore? It is a lie! Now you teach life, the most difficult subject. You did not give up so many positions, you just changed the job descriptions! Your experiences and your strenghts, and even your moments of weakness, are the new mastery that you are dictating. I am your fan and I am not saying your best student because you know how I am... I was always a bad student, but I am sure the president of your fan club! So when you sign autographs I will stand next to you handing you the books. I am proud to have you as my friend, you are great! How much I love you!».

Or this one: «Many years ago, Galeano told this story: "The ginkgo, the oldest of the trees, has been in the world since the time of the dinosaurs. They say that its fan blades relieve asthma, headaches, and the ailments of old age. And it has been proven that these leaves are also the best remedy against a bad memory. When the atomic bomb turned the city of Hiroshima into a desert of blackness, an old Ginkgo was struck down near the center of the explosion. The tree was as charred as the Buddhist temple that the tree protected. Three years later, someone discovered that a little green light was sticking out of the coal. The dead Ginkgo had given an outbreak. The tree was reborn, opened its arms, blossomed. That survivor of the massacre is still there". I think of you. I send you a hug».

Just about to send it for editorial correction, I received the following:

«Oh, Florencia! What a trip! You captured in these words so much, so much, so much, that I don't know if you can dimension it. Undoubtedly a healing path, you say it yourself in the end, how writing was transforming your speech... I read and think: life is magical. It is amazing how pains heal. Those who still cannot see will surely look at you with sorrow, they will only see a broken vase. Those of us who are privileged to see the gold that melts in those cracks, will be eternally grateful for your rich transformation and your generous openness, thank you for being perfectly imperfect!».

I ask myself again: what else can I ask for?

To laugh in the brink of crying

I have been collecting a set of anecdotes, a mixture of black humor with ridiculous situations. I could always laugh at myself, even in contexts of adversity. It is part of what makes me resilient. If this skill managed to survive for the past five years, I believe it has passed the acid test.

It was just a few weeks after my diagnosis when I was appointed to participate in an international meeting in Panama. I received it as a blessing since I needed distance and that unique feeling of being able to look at life from above the clouds. I mentioned it to my great route companion and we discovered that she would be traveling a week later to Mexico. We immediately exchanged glances and devised a plan. We understood each other without the need for words. We did it. We spent a weekend together in a beautiful hotel on the Pacific. I knew that she had been very shocked by my news. The first night we had dinner in a restaurant near the sea, in which there were almost no people... except for a couple who sat next to us and just listened to our conversation with interest throughout the night. I cried the whole time during dinner while my friend listened to me. And the couple, too, obviously. And the waiter too, of course. My friend also had taken care of getting advice and brought me information about two good resources that could help me, and that only when I was able to face them, I looked them up. The next day I went for a coffee at the hotel bar and I found the same waiter from the night before. He recognized me and said: «Madam, today you must enjoy yourself».

I am aware that stiffness affects my face expression. And that in the late afternoon, the accumulation of stress and exhaustion makes me look different. But the last straw was a day when I left the car to be repaired in the morning and went to pick it up in the afternoon. The mechanic argued to my exhaustion that I was not the same person who had left the car!

While I was being attended by a hairdresser, a friend of his approached to talk with him. She told him, concerned, that her husband was being studied for symptoms, which she mentioned. When the friend left, I told the hairdresser: «He may have Parkinson's», and he replied: «Oh, no, how horrible!!».

I went to see an endocrinologist I didn't know. When I told him about my illness, he said: «I can't believe it». When he said goodbye, he said: «I really can't believe it, I loved meeting you».

My brother, while I was trying to get out of his truck: «But you take longer to get off than my mother, who is 70 years old!».

One day I was on my way to give a lecture. I was made up and well-groomed with my papers in hand, ready to review them on the way. I asked for a taxi and when I got up I noticed that there was a cane. I figured if the driver hadn't wanted me to see it he might have hidden it. I put my papers aside. I looked at him, exchanged a few words, and connected with his pain. And since I have lost the fear of asking, I was direct. The man told me about his illness, his fears, and his deep depression, excited that I had become interested in him. I told him about me. We both cried while he said to me: «So...then there is an after...».

PART V

Honeymoon

September 2017 - July 2018

My neurologist had told me that when I began taking levodopa I would feel so good that I would run away, but I never imagined how far. I pushed for the change. It was a difficult decision. Something like... «*You have a certain guarantee that you can count on five years of very good quality of life ahead of you. When do you want them to enjoy them?*».

Under the leadership of chemistry

My neurologist had explained to me the convenience of starting with an initial medication plan that did not include levodopa. He went on to tell me: «in your case, I must think 30 years ahead», referring to how young I was. He explained to me —and I also read— about the frequent side effects of this medication, with the counterpart that for a period of three to five years one practically forgets the disease. This period is called the honeymoon with levodopa.

I wondered a lot how long I should wait before reaching that stage. I was racking my brain trying to decide whether to continue working or not because of the shortage of energy caused by a lack of dopamine. Giving up and having my husband give up on activities, programs, and, ultimately, life as a couple that we both had been enjoying. There came a time when, not knowing if I was doing the right thing, I began to pressure my doctor about the need to move to the next stage. I was 50 years old and did not want to delay the possibility of feeling my best. Would I be making the worst mistake of my life?

When I finally started with the new plan and took a quarter of a levodopa pill as a transition... I transformed myself. Not in a medicated version of me, it was a version of myself from several years ago, that I didn't even remember had existed. I told my husband that it was hard to believe, that maybe I was influenced by the idea of the new treatment, but he replied: «Just look at yourself».

The first thing I noticed was that long-awaited change to free me from the paralyzing apathy. But everything began to improve: the psychic, the motor, and the cognitive abilities. I showed up to work a few days later as someone else. So much so, that I told my new boss: «I introduce myself, I am Florencia Cerruti, you do not know me». A little jokingly, a little seriously, but the truth was that I was not the same one from a few days ago.

I kept tirelessly repeating: «I feel so good». Little by little I noticed my abilities and skills coming back. I stopped needing help with daily tasks, especially cutting food, which so mortified me.

But nostalgia arose, from everything I had delegated when I was not feeling well. The desire to join activities that I had given up. But I had a very fresh feeling of not being able to do everything and I didn't want to be wrong again.

I was amazed by the many effects and consequences the lack of dopamine made me feel; all triggered by a chemical imbalance. So I thought that during all that time I was under the leadership of chemistry. So that wasn't me? Who was I? Which of those versions am I?

My husband must have felt that his wife had been switched twice. He had been playing his caretaker role with absolute dedication. And suddenly, wham!, to rearrange the roles again. I think it was not easy for him to adapt to this latest version.

How do you handle being married to someone so changeable and who will continue to change more? How I wish I could spare him everything he went through and everything that he will have to endure!

Wham!
The fall of the wall of pleasures

I created a space in the garden in front of my house that only lacked some privacy. The dog had won the area behind. After many family discussions, I managed to find a way. We decided that the solution was to place an iron sheet above the front wall of the house. The land has a trapezoidal layout, so it took several meters of sheet metal and a considerable investment. When finished, the blacksmith warned that the wall would have to be reinforced, because there were sections in which the brick was loose. He gave us a budget and we accepted it, although we were not very happy.

And during a weekend I experienced the wonderful sensation of going out to the garden, at dawn, in my pajamas, throwing myself in a hammock to do nothing, with the only whisper of a trio of Poplars for company. And I found myself feeling pleasure. I was surprised by that forgotten feeling.

I repeated a million times how happy I felt. But my happiness lasted as long as a sigh. Two days later, the same night we accepted the blacksmith's estimate, a strong summer storm hit the area. At one o'clock in the morning, I felt a roar that made me jump out of bed. «The wall!», I yelled. The sight was bleak. Twenty meters of the wall on the floor. Brick, fence, and floors included. The exposed house. The investment evaporated. Pleasure turned into frustration.

I could not recover. I couldn't look outside. I didn't want to talk about it. I had scarcely caressed the feeling of fullness for a few hours and it had been unfairly taken from me. My husband said to me: «You have to learn to get up when you fall». And I replied: «And you are telling me?».

It's time to decrypt files

In all this intense process of rediscovering myself, several times I wondered what my mission in life was. I have always admired those who shared with conviction which was theirs. Who has that information? How do you access it? Who can help me decrypt those files?

I had many signs that coincided in one sense: being a teacher, giving a message of hope.

I first heard a Paraguayan pediatrician who had studied tantric numerology, during a job meeting in Buenos Aires. After having analyzed with incredible accuracy my weaknesses, strengths, karma, etc., she addressed what the numbers said about my mission in life. First, she told me: «Be the presence of God on Earth». My eyes must have gone backward because she immediately softened it with something earthlier: «Give a message of hope: if Florencia did it, it is possible to do it».

I had another sign through the tarot. I had not mentioned it before, perhaps because it kept hitting me, but of course, after meeting the Tower Card I wanted to continue. And the second and last question I asked before turning over a new card was: «And what happens next?». Just as I was, devastated and at the same time stunned after knowing the interpretation of the Tower, which perfectly described what I had been experiencing, I met the Master.

This card is called the knowledge card and it is an example for others. It represents the teacher that exists within each of us. It attracts students who want to soak up their energies and feel inspired. A teacher is a guide on the path, but we must walk that path alone. It will lead us, but we will endeavor to move forward.

I also consulted my birth chart. I was very curious about what I might find in it. I was impressed by what I read. My intelligence, creativity, literary ability, and as a speaker stood out. I was defined as a restless, honest, direct, self-taught, leader, and rational woman. Again and again, it repeated that I had been born to be an important woman, to change the world. To help others, to organize groups.

And finally, I reviewed some publications that gave some guidelines on how to identify what each one's mission is. They recommend self-knowledge, identifying what it is that you enjoy doing so much, what is your special ability. Reading these suggestions, I realized that I have nothing to discover, that I had written it in the first chapter: «Nothing gives me more satisfaction than teaching, than interacting with the public. I also really like to write». What am I doing looking to decrypted files?

However, to be a true teacher I have a long way to go. I must learn to go on without the need for recognition, and to feel satisfied knowing that others are nourished by my experience and that they grow by my side and with my support. But my situation led me to a place of less exposure. My reflections are present in the speeches of others. My ideas are put into practice without being acknowledged. Could it be that people think I don't need recognition? Once a friend told me: «Flor, I do not tell you those things that I say to others in the group because I do not consider that you need it». It hurts. It bothers me that it hurts, but I can't help it. I have drowned the crying locked in the bathroom at work and on the pillow while my husband slept. Feelings are ambivalent; I feel protected and I stress less in a position of less exposure. But the pain pierces me and it does not seem fair to transfer it to anyone, because the fight is internal, it is within me, with the area that I do not like to recognize in myself.

I reached out to my near friend who would understand me... I wrote him a Whatsapp text message. «Today I am not well; I am not used to being invisible». Within a minute I had the incredible answer: «I know what it is, I am sure... It is something like doing everything and because of the present situation, you are in the shadows with little recognition. For us, work is like the product of an artist, and art needs recognition». In less than a minute he had written in perfect words what I barely outlined. We agreed to support each other by moving towards giving without waiting for recognition, enjoying the pleasure of giving that we both know how to experience.

I do not doubt that these mixed feelings have a basis in the mourning of the interrupted projects, in having had to give up things that I enjoyed because of the body, the mind and the energy are not with me. It hurts. It hurts a lot.

In addition to giving up what I cannot do, I have been giving up many activities so as not to leave my rehabilitation schedule for early in the morning. I have missed international video conferences, instances that I would have enjoyed, or that would have given me prestige. But I know that I cannot do everything. However, that does not prevent it from hurting so much.

And when the pain pierces, I cling to an answer given by a co-worker to someone who asked about me during an activity that I was unable to attend: «Florencia is like the sun, even if we don't see her, she's always there». Sublime, generous, perfect for my soul in pain. What more can I ask for?

Coming out of the closet

It took me almost five years to break the shell and decide to face the world by openly acknowledging that I had Parkinson's disease. That was 10 percent of my life. It seems like an eternity to me, but it was what it took me.

The first idea to peek out of the closet came from a neighbor's suggestion. She invited me to speak to a group of women in a church about my experiences and what I had been writing about. It was in 2017. I built up my courage and went. I thought that a small group, made up of women who come together to grow spiritually and prepare for life, made an ideal environment to go into the water. But the experience did not turn out exactly as I imagined. The coordinator of the meeting wanted to protect me and did not announce the reason for my presence. And she asked me to introduce myself and to feel free to open up. She asked me several times if I felt comfortable doing it. But I had already accepted the invitation! All that preamble to protect myself shocked me and I began to speak and faltered. We had an incredible exchange, but we all ended up crying and hugging... Today I am still connected with several of these fabulous women.

The second instance was an invitation for an interview in a participatory diagnosis for neurodegenerative diseases. The meeting coordinator got in touch with my boss first, to ask if he could call me. And my boss replied that he would consult me previously. I accepted. I gave my opinion and mentioned all my ideas. I stayed in touch to think about projects together.

But in parallel, I had to find a way of communicating my diagnosis in the different circles of my life. A strange idea came to my mind: to present myself in a literary contest of short stories about Parkinson's organized by an association in Spain. I sent a story I titled *On the Other Side of Fears*, under the pseudonym *Garra Charrúa*. What I was not encouraged to do in my country with people nearby, I did six thousand miles away. Perhaps, confident that no one knew me there. But deep down, knowing that there could be a lot of simpleness in that trust. I let what had to flow, flow. In any case, it wouldn't have been me who decided to spread the word. Perhaps I was waiting for the news to come through without me being responsible.

The result thrilled me to the bone. My story was among the ten finalists and they announced that it would later be included in a book to be published by the association. When I saw the email header that said: «We are pleased to tell you that your story was chosen among the top ten», I was grateful to be home at the time. I couldn't stop crying and shaking uncontrollably.

In turn, I implemented other strategies. At work, I asked the team members I lead and my peers on the management team to be my spokespeople. I explained to them that I no longer wanted to keep my disease from others and that I preferred my diagnosis to be known to those close to me in some way.

A colleague was surprised and asked: «Do you really prefer that everyone knows? Why?». I replied: «Because I'm sick of

172 | REBIRTH AT 50 - FLORENCIA CERRUTI

being asked why I brush my teeth with the electric toothbrush and being snubbed, tired of feeling the disapproving looks when I lie down on the couch, or bored to have a feeling of guilt when I'm late because I went through my morning exercise routine». He looked surprised, but I know he understood me.

In the family, I began to share what I had been writing. I also shared it with one of my husband's best friends.

And in the bathroom, when asked about the electric toothbrush, I began to answer: «I use it because I have stiff hands, I have Parkinson's and I can't wash well with the common one». I am aware that I left more than one woman speechless, but I no longer want to linger around the news.

Then came the gathering of my generation of the Bachelor of Nutrition. A suggestion emerged to celebrate 30 years of our graduation. Most of us had never seen each other again. I had followed a path of the minority, which was that of nutrition policies and on that route, I did not come across any of them. I was struggling thinking how and when to tell them. I might say nothing, because since taking levodopa symptoms are almost not noticeable, but I was thinking about publishing the book and it was strange for me to be with them and not tell them. In the meantime, while I reflected, a colleague shared a poem called *My soul is in a hurry* in the WhatsApp group, which caused each one to tell of a painful part of their life that they had not shared. I told mine. The responses were incredible. And in the meeting, they gave me a space to share as I have rarely had. Now they are waiting for the presentation of the book since that meeting.

Almost simultaneously, I received a visit from my colleague and former co-worker. As I already mentioned, it was thanks to her that I began to contact people with Parkinson's and we founded the group of seven. And with this last project, I came out of the closet, the room, and the house. And I crossed the street.

PART VI

Letters

A friend of mine told me I have a fan in her husband. Now and then he mentions something of what I wrote, and he suggested that I should write about my daughters. It came out in the format of a letter. And I felt it wasn't just one letter that I wanted to write. I cried a lot, really a lot, while I did it. I drained the tears tank, including the reservoir. But at the same time, I felt that I had reached a new milestone: telling my loved ones what my heart was crying out for, but that I didn't dare to put into spoken words. I realized that I was clear about the essential message I wanted to tell each of them and that was stuck in my throat.

Besides, I keep some memories, which I will treasure in my retina and my heart, of the moments when these letters reached their recipients: the image of my mother sitting in the chaos of my creativity corner, reading hers with visible emotion, the wet hug from my husband in the cabin of a boat, the incredible messages from my daughters...

To Gustavo, my husband and lifelong partner

My love,

I always state that you're my source of balance.

It comes to my mind that winter afternoon in 2002, when we were going through the terrible economic crisis that hit us so hard. I remember our conversation in the living room, in which you said to me with emotion: «I know that together we will overcome it», a commitment that we sealed with one of those hugs I will never forget. We sailed through that situation and we could get out of it.

My illness shook us. Impossible to have imagined it. A new challenge that we faced together, and from which we are emerging strengthened.

From you, few words and many actions. When I asked you if you felt fear, anger, or sadness, at least you admitted to me «a little of all that», but you pointed out that the most important thing for you was to act. And I was touched by how you acted.

You assumed the role of protector and caregiver without ever complaining.

Reading testimonies from other caregivers allowed me to stand in your shoes. The possibility that you might feel like some of them, who didn't recognize in their partner the person they had chosen to share the rest of their lives, horrified me. And I feel that you have the right to think that your wife has been changed... and to claim for the deceit!

I will do my best to keep being your wife, despite having become a different one. Perhaps in some ways, I am less unbearable...

I will not lie to you. I'm terrified of what might come and I try not to think about it because I can't even know if it will happen. But I do know I don't want you to become my nurse. I have already overused your love and kindness. I want you to take care of yourself, have time for yourself, and enjoy your life.

Help me live in the now. Together at your side, I feel safe.

Thank you for your unconditional love each day.

I adore you.

Florencia

To my daughters, Elisa and Sofía

To my «little girls»:

You'll always be my «little girls» to me, although people joke about this.

I still remember something you told me when you were kids: «Nothing is enough for you». I listen to these words while I realize it must have not been easy for you to have such a strict, controlling, and perfectionist mother. My world turned over when I learned I had Parkinson's disease. The diagnosis forced me to rethink absolutely everything. It was a process of deep growth, as well as a very intense and painful one. In that process, I was in great need to quit being a mother for a while and I let your dad take care of everything. I couldn't handle that «everything» myself; I hope someday you will understand.

It is not easy for me to accept being taken care of. But I'm moved when I see your care and affection while doing so. When one of you offers to cut my food, or when the other helps me get dressed whenever she sees me getting nervous running late.

I am very proud of you as I see you grow and become whole women. I believe that having to deal with adversity and disability will give you skills for life. I am also convinced that jointly we will enjoy this new mother that has come up out of this intense process.

However, I must confess that this is not what I would have chosen for you. I am so scared to think I might embarrass you in front of your friends. But I must recognize that I've seen you handle with integrity my anxiety episodes, like when you found me pulling the weeds out in the garden at midnight with my miner flashlight, or when you got back from your night out at six a.m…

I want you to know that sometimes the chemistry overrules me and the real me finds it hard to manifest. But I also want you to always remember that despite this and whichever symptom appears, my love for you does nothing else but grow.

You're my greatest legacy to this world. Your dad and I must have done something right for both of you to have such bulletproof self-esteem. I love seeing you in harmony with your boyfriends and surrounded by friends. I enjoy watching you thrive in your lives and being solid partners with your boyfriends. I am at peace knowing that you have absolutely everything you need to be happy.

Be happy.

Love,

Mom

To my mother

Beloved Mommy:

In this major challenge we both have to face, your unconditional love played a crucial role. I knew that I had to start over, and that whatever version of me emerged, you will accept and love me.

You have told me that you are fully aware that your mission in life is to go along with others. I remember dad's laughter when I called you on the phone to ask you to join me somewhere and you accepted immediately, without even being very clear about where we were going or what we would do.

You accomplished your mission. You performed your role as a companion with wisdom like no one else, as if you knew me from the deepest place of my insides, capturing what I didn't understand, guessing what I was thinking and feeling, even if I didn't say it.

It took me six months to answer your words: «I'm not ready to see you suffer». I couldn't stop standing in your shoes, because it's inherent to motherhood to see that our children don't suffer. But I was also going through the stage in which I was running out of fuel and it was difficult for me to face any additional effort. But when I felt better and took up therapy again, I saw it so clear and so easy. And that little conversation we had a few days ago gave me infinite peace.

As I told you, your daughter doesn't suffer; she just has some discomforts... who doesn't? Also, she follows your example. You can't imagine how much I admire you for not always complaining when you are not feeling well. So you can't be surprised that I didn't tell you how bad I felt. I learned it from you.

Your daughter doesn't suffer; she is learning like never in her life, and she is looking at growing into a new version of herself. This is also your daughter, who feels that she has started anew and who was lucky that her mother was present and willing to be with her while she rebirths and to welcome her unconditionally in her new version.

Both of us will indeed have to mourn for the version of Florencia that is now gone, for the interrupted projects, for the aborted races, for the unfulfilled goals, for the bonds that are no longer there. But as St. Augustine said: «Happiness consists in taking with joy what life gives us and in letting go with the same joy what life takes from us». That was one of the greatest lessons I take from this process for the rest of my life. When I learned to let go I could understand that everything happens for some reason, and I found that I feel much more in harmony in this new version.

One and a thousand times more... thank you, Mommy! I hope someday my daughters will feel for me a bit of what I feel for you.

Florencia

To you, who are on my same path

Perhaps you feel like me, faced with the greatest challenge life has ever set before you. You will ask yourself thousands of questions. The most difficult to answer is probably: «How am I supposed to go on?». What I can tell you is that there is life after the diagnosis of a neurodegenerative disease and that this depends immensely on your attitude. Easy? No, very difficult. But it is possible. You will indeed have hundreds of fears. But you will also have some resources on which to rely on to get started. What do I mean? For example, people who love you unconditionally, personal resources such as perseverance, intelligence, resilience, or the capacity of self-motivation, other resources that can be useful in this setting. Then... identify them and begin. One step at a time. Day by day. Don't freeze, don't sink, don't give up!

I don't have the magic recipe you'd probably want to find. But I can tell you some things that I learned and that helped me, that might give you relief or inspiration.

Wait! There's no need to rush about some things. Don't hurry to spread the news. Many things that can ease or make the process harder will depend on when and how you do it. Don't rush to make drastic decisions at work. Especially if you are feeling very down. There will be days in which you would prefer to hide your head under the ground, not see anyone and shelter in your house, but not every day will be like this. Look for advice before making a decision. Give yourself time to stabilize and do a thorough analysis.

Choose your professional army. It will be a long journey together. You must be able to trust them blindly and feel that they listen to you. It doesn't matter that they are the most renowned. Although it is good that you choose among those who have specialized in the disease. Many professionals have had practically no contact with Parkinson's, and especially with early-onset patients.

Listen to your body. No one knows it better than you do. You're the one who can best say whether you are comfortable with a treatment or not. About whether it's enough or not. Don't take the first no. Insist! If you are convinced that something is wrong, bring it up again or consult someone else.

Trust your intuition. You will have to make decisions all the time. Seek advice from those who know and love you. Pick up the antennas and watch for signals. They will help you find your way. Make proposals to your army that you feel will work. Finally, you decide and guide your treatment.

Listen to your heart. As a friend once said to me: «You can argue with me about what I think, but not what I feel». You will shed tears of pain, of anger, of sadness, of injustice, but also of emotion. Permit yourself to let them run. You will see that the tears of emotion are finally winning. Don't you feel any of this? I find it hard to believe; you may have to dive deeper.

Give yourself time to go through each stage. Only you know when you're ready to close one and consider another milestone. You'll meet a lot of people who think differently and encourage you to move faster with the best intention, don't worry. But listen to the rumble to react when they come from those who love you or from a specialist.

Let yourself be loved, pampered, and helped. Many people don't come close because they're afraid or don't know how to do it. Give them some sign that their support is welcome. And if you are clear about the best way they can help you, let them know it.

Find out your poisons and antidotes. If you have Parkinson's, remember that each person develops a unique set of symptoms and that what works for others may not work for you or vice versa. In my experience, besides complying strictly with the medication prescribed by the doctor, three things do not fail: exercise, meditation, and sleep. So essential that it is scary: moving, breathing, and resting. When you have Parkinson's, these things may make your day change.

Don't over demand yourself... it's better to move slowly but steadily. Remember that the secret is in the breaks. Begin to walk the path, check how you feel, and go on the way you think is best.

You are not alone! When you feel it is time, try to meet people who are going through the same thing as you. But they should be in a similar stage of life and illness. You will experience a magical effect.

A matter of attitude. As I was saying, don't place on others the responsibility for what happens to you. Your attitude is crucial in many aspects. You can decide to live this process as a great opportunity, to reinvent yourself, to start over, to rebirth or – as Sean Buranahiran says – to move up to the next level of your life.

Easy? No! Very difficult! But not impossible. I wish you success in whatever you decide!

Someone like you

P.S.: And I say goodbye sharing this text by Sean Buranahiran which was the most beautiful and inspiring thing I've read in recent times.

When a bowl is broken in Japan, it is put back together with the cracks being filled with gold, creating a beautiful lining. This is to emphasize the beauty in what was once broken. They believe that when something has suffered damage and has a history it makes it more beautiful and the same goes for human beings.

Everything that you've been through and everything you're going through doesn't make your life uglier although it may seem that way when we're going through it. It's up to us to choose to paint our struggles with gold and make it beautiful. You are not broken and beyond repair. You can pick yourself up and learn from what's happened and become a better person because of the struggle that you`ve been through. You can wear your scars proudly as a badge of honor, as if to say: «Look what I've been through! It made me who I am today, and I can get through anything life puts in front of me now».

Nobody has had a perfect life and nobody ever will. It's only up to us if we choose to paint our broken pieces gold and make them beautiful. Don't be ashamed of what you've been through, everything that's happened to you has been for a reason. So the more we deny it, the more we complain and don't accept what's happened to us, the less it becomes useful to us. The moment we accept and find that what´s useful in the struggle, the things that we´ve been through, that's just like painting the cracks in our broken pieces gold, turning something that could be ugly into something beautiful and inspiring. When what you've been through is an inspiration for other people, then it was all worth it. So don't get stacked on how things used to be.

I once heard a quote that said: «Every next level of your life will demand a new version of you». And sometimes it takes being broken to become that new version of yourself. So if you're going through bad times, I hope these words can help you or someone you love.

Final words

It's been four years since I started writing.

Some have told me that in these pages perhaps I idealize some situations, or that I am still a perfectionist and not very humble person... I don't deny that this is the case. But what I do not doubt is that there was a before and an after the diagnosis, a new beginning, a start anew. Honestly, I didn't find an alternative path.

I re-read what I have finished writing and I notice a shift. The first chapters are an urgent request for someone to understand and help me, and to understand myself, but as the pages run they turn into a: «Can I help you?». I began to write asking for help and understanding; I ended up offering knowledge and skills, but also help and understanding.

I don't know if this is the end of the beginning or the beginning of the end. I don't know if the adverse effects of levodopa will come. Perhaps they will discover a cure for the disease. Maybe I'll write again. Sometimes I find myself fancying being able to publish an upcoming book entitled: *I was cured of Parkinson's disease*. I am now 52 years old and, perhaps in the future, I can benefit from some of the several research studies that are currently running worldwide in different areas of focus.

As of now, I am capitalizing on huge baggage of knowledge. I learned that life does not end the day you are diagnosed with a neurodegenerative disease; a new one begins. I learned to let go, not to want to control everything, to feel vulnerable, and to connect with those who feel the same way, and that there is always a half-full glass to hold on to.

In the meantime, I try to live in the present and enjoy this honeymoon. I remember what the poem says: «Because every day is a new beginning, because this is the hour and the best moment».

To all those who have patiently and unconditionally been at my side during these five years, thousands of thanks.

To the angels who showed up when I most needed them, infinite thanks. They know who they are.

To those who joined me along the way and encouraged me to publish these pages, here they are: mission accomplished. They also know who they are.

Glossary of Uruguayan terms

The *rambla* is an avenue that goes along the entire coastline of Montevideo, the capital of Uruguay. As an integral part of Montevidean identity, it's a very important site for recreation and leisure. Every day, a large number of people go there to take long strolls, jog, bicycle, roller skate, fish and even – in a special area – skateboard. Its 17 miles' length makes it one of the longest esplanades in the world.

Mate is a traditional drink in Uruguay. The drink, which contains mateine (an analog of caffeine), is made by an infusion of dried leaves of yerba mate. It is usually drunk with friends and served in a hollow calabash gourd with a «bombilla», a special metallic drinking straw. The gourd is known as a mate. Even if the water comes in a very modern thermos, the drink is traditionally drunk from mates. Like other brewed herbs, yerba mate leaves are dried, chopped, and ground into a powder called yerba. The bombilla is both a straw and a sieve. The end which is placed in the drink is wider, with small holes or slots that let the brewed liquid in, but block the chunky matter that makes up much of the mixture.

«**Garra charrúa**» is a term used to express that the Uruguayan has an innate condition of bravery, which makes him overcome any adversity by force of courage.

About the author

Florencia Cerruti was born in Montevideo, Uruguay in 1966. She holds a master's degree in Nutrition and has promoted child well-being through several books and articles throughout three decades working passionately for early childhood policies. A natural optimistic warrior, she decides, after 5 years of her Parkinson's diagnosis, to face the world to help others through her experience. In 2018 her story was published as one of the ten finalists in the Parkinson's Association of Astorga literary contest, Spain. Her book was exhibited in the 2019 Parkinson's World Congress in Kyoto, Japan.

Follow the author

I love to be in touch with my readers.

www.florencia.cerruti.com

renaceralos50@gmail.com

www.facebook.com/renaceralos50

Florencia Cerruti in youtube

@renacer a los 50 in instagram

Printed in Great Britain
by Amazon

49591738R00113